Divine Reflections

in Natural Phenomena

Eva Peck

© 2013 by Eva Peck

All rights reserved

Except for any fair dealing permitted under the Copyright Act, no part of this book may be reproduced by any means without prior permission of the author and publisher.

Photography: Alexander Peck with the exception of:
Page 35 which is courtesy of http://www.freedigitalphotos.net and page 114 which is the credit of Jindrich Degen

Cover and graphic design: Eva Peck

Bible verses taken from the HOLY BIBLE, NEW INTERNATIONAL VERSION. Copyright © 1973, 1978, 1984 by International Bible Society. Used by permission of Zondervan Publishing House. All rights reserved.

National Library of Australia Cataloguing-in-Publication entry

Author: Peck, Eva.
Title: Divine reflections in natural phenomena / Eva Peck; Alexander Peck, photography.

ISBN: 9780987090591 (pbk.)

Subjects: Nature--Religious aspects.
         Spiritual formation.
         Spiritual life.

Other Authors/Contributors: Peck, Alexander.

Dewey Number: 248.2

The book can be purchased online through
www.heavens-reflections.org or www.pathway-publishing.org

Dedicated to the One
in whom we live, move and have our being,
and to those desiring, as well those who do not yet desire,
to perceive the Divine in all things.

Other Books by the Same Author

Divine Reflections in Times and Seasons
Divine Reflections in Living Things
Divine Insights from Human Life

Co-author of:
Pathway to Life – Through the Holy Scriptures
Journey to the Divine Within – Through Silence, Stillness and Simplicity

Acknowledgments

First, I would like to thank the Great God for enabling, inspiring and blessing this publication.

I must also thank my husband, Alex, for his encouragement and support. He is always ready to help with editing and to give helpful advice. Without his valuable input, this book would not have come out as it has.

CONTENTS

Preface 9

Introduction 12

Order, Beauty and Harmony 16
    Chance or Design? 16
    Laws of Conservation 18
    Clocks and Internal Programs 19
    Harmony and Beauty 20
    Display of Divine Character 22
    Disruption and Restoration 25

Of Creations and Creators 29
    Contrast to Divine Creation 31
    Other Contrasting Creations 32

Life's Paradoxes and Mysteries 35
    World of Paradoxes 36
    Possible Answers 37
    Future Hope 39

Life and Death 41
    The Marvel of Life 43
    Humanity in the Web of Life 44
    Ultimate Life and Death 46
    The Source of Life 50
    Raised to Life 52
    Life and Death Struggle 54

Weather 58
    Effects of Weather 59
    Weather and Life Seasons 60
    Biblical Weather Metaphors 61

Weather and Humanity 63

The Heavens and the Earth 66

The Heavens 68
The Seas 70
The Dry Land 72
Built-In Adversity 73

The Marvel of Water 76

Unique and Indispensible 77
Holy Spirit – the Living Water 80

Riverside Reflections 88

Rivers and Their Environs.. 89
Life as a River 92
Spiritual Analogies of a River 97

Springs in the Desert 99

Deserts in the Bible 100
Life as a Desert Experience 101
Spiritual Parallels 103

From Deserts to Oceans... 105

Water as Type of the Holy Spirit 106
The Spirit – Past to Future 108

About the Author 114

More About the Author's Other Books..................... 116

Other Resources 118

Readers' Comments 120

About Pathway Publishing 123

Preface

Since early childhood, I have been captivated by the natural world. From blossoms in spring, buds opening into leaves, butterflies fluttering from one flower to the next, earthworms and caterpillars crawling on the ground, to the occasional hare or deer I would sight on family outings away from the city of Prague – all this and more fascinated me. It was why I chose to study science in high school and later at university. Even now on nature walks with my husband and father, I'm often the first to spot lorikeets in a tree hole, a wallaby in the bushes, a koala high up on a eucalyptus tree, or an unusual flower, mushroom or lizard along the path.

While nature has always spoken to me, it was only in my late teens that God opened my mind to his existence. At that time, nature took on an even deeper meaning as I could now see behind everything a Designer, Creator, Life-giver and Sustainer. Mindless, haphazard evolution no longer made sense as an answer to the order, harmony and complexity of the natural world. For a long time, I rejected the idea of evolution altogether, believing in a special divine creation as described in the Bible. However, as I have continued to read on the subject, I couldn't deny the massive amount of evidence for an evolutionary origin of life on earth. As with many things, I have come to the conclusion that the truth must incorporate and hold in tension both alternatives – a Mind behind all things (the immanent nature of the Divine in which "we [and all that exists] live and move and have our being" – Acts 17:28), as well as natural and evolutionary processes ultimately accomplishing divine purposes.

As I became more acquainted with the message of the Bible, I began to perceive in natural phenomena a picture of spiritual realities. These insights became the genesis of this book which is the second of a trilogy. The other two are *Divine Reflections in Times and Seasons* and *Divine Reflections in Living Things* (both available through www.pathway-publishing.org and www.heavens-reflections.org).

Divine Reflections in Natural Phenomena and its companion titles nudge us to take a fresh look at the physical world around us – to see every process and each creature in a new way. The biblical writers, too, point us to the natural world to perceive divine glories (take a look at Psalm 19, for example). If we can pause for a moment and ponder, life and the world around us will begin to unmask such divine qualities as love, wisdom, peace, joy and power before our eyes.

Preface

While this book is based on the belief that God or a Higher Mind is behind all that exists, I do not insist on the literal interpretation of all biblical accounts, as I have come to understand that the Scriptures are not intended to be a strictly scientific or historical work. The assumption is, however, that biblical accounts reveal, sometimes in symbolic language, God's deeds in human history and also point to unseen spiritual realities. Often poetry and metaphor are the best or only vehicles to communicate what is inexpressible in literal language.

I understand that the Divine is neither male nor female. However, to use the pronoun "it" seems inappropriate, therefore I am opting for the grammatical gender "he".

For those drawn to learn more about the biblical teachings behind the observations, footnotes provide scriptural references for the conclusions reached.

Of course, other writers have also expressed the idea that the physical world pictures spiritual realities – each in their own unique way. These are my perceptions based on my experiences and understanding of how certain natural occurrences can be viewed in spiritual terms. May you too gain new insights as you take a fresh look at the seemingly ordinary aspects of your life.

Eva Peck

Introduction

> Where can I go from your Spirit?
> Where can I flee from your presence?
> Psalm 139:7

> He is not far from each one of us.
> 'For in him we live and move and have our being.'
> Acts 17:27-28

The Divine is understood by religious traditions to be transcendent, immanent and personal. Various faiths may emphasise one of these aspects over the others. In the East, for example in India, religion is largely a matter of direct experience and a sense of the sacred is everywhere. In the West, by contrast, correct teachings and beliefs have often been the point of focus.

Few would question the importance of sound teachings. Nevertheless, God is far outside of our realm of perception and comprehension, and therefore human language becomes limited in accurately formulating concepts about the Divine. While groups differ in how they see the Ultimate Reality, no one can know fully in this life – we all understand partially at best.

The Bible includes both doctrinal teachings and references to direct experiences with God. They are presented from individual perspectives of the writers and editors of the Scriptures. From the texts we can deduce that a close, experiential relationship with the Divine is possible. For example, King David is described as a man after God's own heart, Abraham and Job were friends of God, and Enoch and Noah walked with God.[1]

In addition, mystical writers throughout Christian history – as well as those of other religious traditions – have left us records of their unique and intimate bond with the Divine. We are all children of God, each with a special and individual relationship to our Father / Mother (since God is genderless and has both male and female qualities).

This book (the second of a trilogy) suggests that the Divine can be experienced all around us – that indeed everything is sacred and as such teaches us about and brings us closer to God. In other words, the immanent aspect of the Divine pervades all things, enabling us to catch glimpses of the transcendent reality. Increased consciousness of the Creator in the seemingly ordinary and mundane will help us appreciate divine qualities in the creation. Furthermore, it will awaken our own creative potential, since we are not only in God (as is all that exists), but

---

[1] Genesis 5:22-24; 6:9; 2 Chronicles 20:7; Job 29:4; Acts 13:22; James 2:23

are also made in the divine image and therefore co-workers and co-creators with God![2]

For centuries, nature has been seen by many as the second book of divine revelation, next to inspired writings. Through nature we can, by grace, unexpectedly and often in surprising ways, encounter the Divine. When this happens, the literal becomes a metaphor which invites us to explore its larger and deeper meanings. By looking for the sacred in the mundane, be it dew on the grass, clouds in the sky, or new growth in the spring, we can also perceive the interconnection ("inter-being") of all things. Everything contains all else – the sun and clouds are in the grass and buds, which couldn't come into existence without rain and sunshine.

By our becoming open to new possibilities and interpreting experiences in fresh ways, the ordinary becomes transformed into the extraordinary, and what we had previously not even noticed becomes wonderful. When we open our hearts and become emotionally receptive, we will notice surprising presences.

Today, after reading these words, why not make a personal commitment to slow down in order to awaken to the marvels of the natural world. Sit on the

---

[2] Genesis 1:26-27; 1 Corinthians 3:9; 2 Corinthians 6:1; 1 Thessalonians 3:2

Introduction

grass under a tree or on a park bench and look closely at what is around you, using the eyes and ears of both the head and heart. Become focused, giving close attention to what you see. Delight in the diversity of all things – the colours, sounds, smells, shapes and textures. In the richness of life, the creation is filled with inspiration.

Seek to be really aware, mindful and attentive to your surroundings. Open your senses, take a deep look, and truly experience things. Pay closer attention to the unusual flower or beetle, appreciate the beauty and diversity of both the living and non-living aspects of the creation. "Come and see", as the Scriptures encourage.[3] Become open to the unpredictable, to adventure – allow circumstances to spontaneously unfold. Then you, too, may well echo the words of the poet Gerald Manley Hopkins, "The world is charged with the grandeur of God."

---

[3] Psalm 46:8; 66:5; Isaiah 66:18; Matthew 28:6; John 1:46; 4:29; 11:34

Order, Beauty and Harmony

Rows of apple, pear and cherry trees in white and pink blossoms under a cloudless blue sky, the orchard was in full bloom. Bees buzzed from one flower to the next gathering nectar. Sun rays reflected from a nearby pond surface and ducks basked in the warmth of the spring morning. A tabby cat explored the grassy meadow, looking for mice. Poplar trees, dressed in fresh green foliage, swayed gently in the breeze. Recent swallow arrivals returned to their old nests or were busily building new ones, and a blackbird sang heartily. The stork had returned to her old nest on the chimney top and surveyed the breathtaking scene.

Chance or Design?

At some point in the distant past, the universe, including planet Earth and all that is on it, came into being. No one knows exactly when and how, but we can marvel at its complexity, diversity, order and beauty. Ponder, for example, the adaptation of organisms to existing conditions, the complex functions taking place with infinite precision, and the delicate balance in nature (only relatively recently disrupted by human activities).

Considering the intricacy of just one cell is astounding. When one takes into account that millions of cells form the numerous organs performing hundreds if not thousands of functions in a living creature, it becomes mindboggling. Multiply this further by the number of species comprising land, sea and air creatures (including all insects and microorganisms). Add to this the interdependence of all living things and the factors affecting environment and climate, as well as the enormously vast and complex universe beyond our planet (in comparison to which the Earth is like a speck of dust).

Indeed, the natural world is awe-inspiring. Even in today's scientific and technological world, a great deal about the mystery of life is not understood. While not an absolute proof in themselves, the abovementioned phenomena in their incredible intricacy and complexity provide evidence to support the biblical account of a Being or Mind of supreme intelligence and wisdom behind all that exists.[4] When all is taken

---

[4] Job 12:7-10; Psalm 104:5-30; 148:1-12; Nehemiah 9:6; Revelation 14:7; Psalm 10:4; 14:1

into consideration, the probability of everything evolving by mere coincidence or blind chance, without any design, forethought or guidance becomes infinitesimal. Some have stated that in reality more faith is needed to believe in blind evolution than in the existence of a Creator.

Laws of Conservation

Everything visible operates according to principles of law, order and conservation, and is therefore quite predictable. (At the sub-atomic level, processes become considerably more complicated and are far from fully understood.)

Species produce offspring in their own likeness and seeds germinate into the plants or trees they came from. Life cycles continue predictably from birth, via maturing and reproduction, to death. Energy and matter are conserved through natural cycles – for example, water, carbon and nitrogen cycles. Living organisms absorb elements from the air or soil, use them as building blocks or for fuel, and excrete them again, thus returning them into the environment. Cells change continually, aging, dying and being replaced. Everything is interconnected.

A delicate balance and harmony are essential for the proper functioning of all aspects of life. Whenever the order and balance are disrupted – most often through destructive human activities motivated by greed and selfishness – problems result. These may manifest themselves, for example, in upset weather, natural disasters, physical disease, mental illness, relational problems, and premature death.

Clocks and Internal Programs

The universe is like an intricate time machine with myriads of clocks regulating innumerable activities. The Earth, for example, turns around its axis every 24 hours and around the sun every 365¼ days. The sun and moon rise and set according to preset timers. Seasons come and go with their associated weather patterns. Tides go in and out with regularity.

The animate world also abounds with evidence of inbuilt clocks. For example, swallows migrate thousands of kilometres before winter. They leave their European nesting grounds at the same time every year, fly to the same destination in Africa, and return again in the spring to where they came from.

Salmon also have astounding migratory habits built into their life cycle. They hatch and spend their early life stages in fresh water. In their second year, they swim down the river to the ocean where they grow to adult size. Toward the end of their life, between ages four and seven, the fish make a final journey of several thousand kilometres across the ocean, back to the river estuary where their life began to secure the next generation before dying.

Flowers start blossoming at more or less the same time each year. Likewise, fruit ripens and leaves fall according to an inner timing. Young animals and human babies leave the womb after predictable periods of time that are the same for all the members of a species. Birds know how long to sit on their eggs and what to do when the eggs hatch. They understand how and when to teach their young to fly and to prepare them for life – be it in a local area or including long migratory journeys.

Within the bodies of humans and other creatures, all organs work together without the control or even awareness of their "owners". In "social" species, such as ants, bees, wolves and geese, there is order and cooperation, each group member knowing its role and tasks for the benefit and preservation of the others. All functions are predictable, occur in a timely way, and follow internal programming or instinct.

Harmony and Beauty

Like in a beautiful symphony, there is harmony throughout the natural world. Interdependence and cooperation occur everywhere. The countless life forms and natural cycles are intertwined and balanced (barring unwise human intervention). Although struggle and death also take place, they serve to maintain equilibrium and keep the natural cycles going.

Not only is everything in the natural world balanced and functional, but beauty also surrounds us. Consider the harmony of the colours. The world is not just black and white with shades of grey, but is filled with bright as well as muted, well-coordinated colours in marvellous variety. With its basic colours of blue and green, the natural environment has a calming, rejuvenating and balancing effect on the mind, heart and body. Splashes of red, yellow, orange, pink, purple and brown add interest as well as promoting feelings of cheer, serenity, inspiration and vitality, among others.

The natural beauty, aesthetically pleasing to the senses, brings happiness, enjoyment, and even a-musement. We admire the delicate shape of a violet, orchid, or cherry blossom; the yellow carpet of a dandelion-covered meadow; and even the purple flower of a prickly thistle visited by a furry bumblebee. Who can help but smile at kittens, cubs or puppies playing; or hungry chicks with their beaks wide open for mother to drop something in? Before each of us lies a seemingly endless variety of delightful living and non-living things for our eyes to take pleasure in. If only we can pause to admire and smell the lilacs, to explore the forest path, to climb the mountain, to listen to the waves on the seashore.

Display of Divine Character

As a piece of art communicates about the artist, the natural world attests to the qualities and character of the Creator. One can discern love, joy, peace, kindness, gentleness, and patience as well as humility, wisdom, generosity, and imagination throughout the physical world.[5]

Divine love appears in the abundance of good things surrounding us, such as warm spring sunshine, a cool fresh breeze, sweet juicy strawberries, and tender parental care. The creation reflects wonderful benevolence. Barring humanity's destructive deeds, nature functions harmoniously. Furthermore, the Creator's care and provision are unconditionally available to all creatures. While effort and struggle may be required for survival, all organisms are well equipped for life in whatever circumstances they find themselves.[6]

Nature displays joy and even humour – birds chirping, lambs frolicking and exploring their world, human mothers excited about the first smile of their

---

[5] Psalm 104:24; Proverbs 3:19-20; Jeremiah 51:15; Galatians 5:23-25
[6] Matthew 5:45; Luke 6:35

baby. How can we not be amused by kittens hitting each other with their paws as they enforce their "social order", or a puppy barking at a bug? Or, who doesn't enjoy watching toddlers at their first attempts to pull themselves up on the coffee table, discovering what it feels like standing on their feet? Light-heartedness and playfulness abound among living creatures.

Away from the hustle and bustle of human rushing, peace and tranquillity come to the fore. Walking in a forest, for instance, one feels refreshed by the soothing greenery, cool shade, and soft scents. Generally, animals are quiet or make non-disturbing noises. Most birds sing pleasantly, insect buzzing is usually not irritating, and neither is the croaking of frogs. Dogs, cows and other animals only make on-going bothersome noises when upset or unhappy.

Overall, nature's design has inbuilt gentleness. Under normal conditions, climate remains balanced and pleasant, with hurricanes, tornadoes and violent storms being more the exception than the rule. Destructive earthquakes and volcanic eruptions are only occasional occurrences. Most animals are non-aggressive to humans and attack only if threatened or if human activity encroaches on their habitat. Predators are in a minority and usually only kill for food to survive. In addition, they are a vital part of ecosystems and if absent, the other animals tend to overpopulate and become destructive to the environment. In the past century or two, however, the balance in nature has become seriously disrupted by imprudent human activities, and consequently violent natural phenomena are on the rise.

Patience can also be seen in nature's design. In the animal kingdom, creatures patiently wait for their young to hatch and grow up, sometimes under adverse conditions, for which they are equipped. Male emperor penguins, for example, endure weeks of frost and blizzard without eating, huddled together, each with an egg on his feet, waiting for the young to hatch, the spring to arrive, and their female partners to return from feeding in the sea.

Even though God is supreme, sovereign and omnipotent, his awe-inspiring handiwork demonstrates humility – its inherent power is not flaunted before humans. Mighty displays of power in nature through such occurrences as deafening thunder, blinding lightning, or terrifying tsunamis are relatively rare. Instead, a quiet display of wisdom, glory, and generosity occurs in sunrises and sunsets, starry and moonlit nights, and the myriads of living organisms of direct benefit to humans.[7]

---

[7] Psalm 19:1-6; Proverbs 6:6-8

The imagination of the Creator is seen in the astounding variety of designs, sizes, and colour combinations. How many shapes of leaves, types of flowers, kinds of seed "containers", and ways of seed dispersal are there? How many different beaks, flying habits, and nest types come to mind? What about the various sounds that animals produce to communicate with each other, many inaudible to the human ear? Sizes in the animal world range from the 30-metre long and over 100 tons in weight blue whale, to microscopic organisms visible only under electron microscope. The plant kingdom at its large end features the 100 metres tall giant sequoias with a base diameter of 10 metres. These trees and the whales make humans look miniature in comparison. All this is, however, dwarfed, by incredible heavenly phenomena such as the billions of galaxies of which the Milky Way is only a tiny part.

Disruption and Restoration

Humans are the only creatures on the earth who have been endowed with free moral agency. Created in divine image and given stewardship (not ownership or licence to exploit) over the rest of the natural world, we are in a special position. Our nature, however, has been marred by what has been referred to as the Fall – the choice made by our ancestors in primeval history to go contrary to their Maker.[8]

Estranged from God, human nature is not subject to divine teaching and is a paradoxical mixture of good and evil. While men and women can create inspiring art, compose near-celestial music, and perform sacrificial deeds, a dark side also lurks, described in the Bible as the "acts of the sinful nature" or "works of the flesh". Others use the term "ego". This accounts for traits such as selfishness, unfaithfulness, intemperance, intolerance, strife, envy, jealousy, greed, anger, hatred, rebellion and murder.[9]

The global balance and harmony has been disrupted by human disregard for what has been divinely ordained. As a result, pain and suffering have entered – sickness and disease on the individual level; war, poverty and famine on the national level; and destructive natural disasters on the global level. Physical and spiritual laws governing life, when ignored or neglected, bring about adverse consequences – the law of cause and effect too is in operation (referred to by Buddhists as karma). While forbearance, mercy and patience operate in the universe, justice and judgment are also present.[10]

---

[8] Genesis 1:26; 3:1-24
[9] Romans 7:18-23; Galatians 5:19-21
[10] Leviticus 26:3-45; Deuteronomy 28:1-68; Proverbs 22:8-9; 2 Corinthians 9:6; Galatians 6:7-9; Exodus 34:6-7

Although cause and effect as well as order and predictability overall exist, in the human life this doesn't always appear to work. Sometimes unexpected and unexplainable suffering comes to those who have done all in their power to follow a right way of life. Conversely, a person who does evil is seemingly getting away with it or even appears to prosper.

The biblical story of Job portrays a just man unjustly afflicted, thus overturning the notion that humans can control their destiny by their behaviour. At the end of the story, God reveals himself as the Creator who does great, mysterious and incomprehensible things for divine reasons.[11]

The book of Ecclesiastes shows the futility of trying to fully understand life, but advises trusting and remaining faithful to God regardless of the apparent injustices or meaninglessness.[12] Some of the psalmists and prophets also lamented about the seeming gross injustices. They were, however, reassured that in the end justice would prevail.[13]

In infinite and unfathomable wisdom, God has created an ordered universe (even though the law of chaos also operates) and allowed humans, made in

---

[11] Job 12:4-6; 21:7-26; 38:1-42:3
[12] Ecclesiastes 1:2-11; 11:5; 12:13-14
[13] Psalm 37:1-40; 73:3-28; 94:3-23; Malachi 3:15-18; Habakkuk 1:13-17; 2:1-20

divine image and given freedom of choice, a limited control over it. The Creator has given people a desire to know how the universe works as well as to understand their lives in relation to it, to each other, and to God. While we have been able to discover a great deal about our world and universe through scientific exploration, a large amount still eludes us. In this life, ultimate understanding that surpasses human reason is unavailable to humans except through special revelation, but even then much for now remains awe-inspiring mystery.[14]

The Bible, however, gives a wonderful hope. A time is coming when the Creator and all humanity will be reconciled. There will also be restoration and renewal of the universe. Then too new knowledge will be revealed and previous mysteries understood. A pristine heaven and earth will emerge with an order, beauty and harmony that will pale today's world into insignificance.[15]

---

[14] Deuteronomy 29:29; Job 5:9; 9:10-12; 37:5; 42:3; Psalm 145:3; Romans 11:33; 1 Corinthians 2:6-14; 13:9-12

[15] Acts 3:21; Romans 8:19-24; 2 Peter 3:13; Revelation 21:1-4; Isaiah 11:6-10

Of Creations and Creators

The sun had barely risen, casting a pink hue on the desert countryside. Tops of rocks illuminated by the sunlight contrasted with the surrounding shady areas. Some of the rock formations were reminiscent of large skulls, perhaps not unlike those at Golgotha where Jesus' crucifixion took place. Walking over stony paths and then through cultivated parks, we marvelled at God's creation – as well as man's. Nature had provided the building blocks and people arranged them to create parks and gardens. Even the human ability to think aesthetically, to design, and to bring plans into reality is God given.

According to the Genesis creation story, God personally sculpted the first man from soil, making him in his image and then breathing life into him. Like God, each person is in their unique way a creator. In fact, we are all co-creators with the Divine. Endowed with creative abilities and inspired, humans can produce remarkable works of art and beauty. Often drawing on ideas and insights from nature and utilizing what God created for materials, they plant picturesque gardens, construct impressive buildings, and develop technological wonders.[16]

On our walk, we were awed by the seemingly ordinary things in nature – the symmetry and magnificence of each date palm; a desert bush with green fruit in the shape and size of tennis balls; and the various shades of green of the palms, wattles, eucalypti, shrubs, plants and grasses. Also fascinating were the leaf shapes varying from round to oval to heart-shaped to kidney-shaped, to long and narrow, to short and tiny. Equally amazing was the range of textures – soft, firm, smooth, coarse, hairy and velvety. Flowers in diverse sizes, shapes and colours provided splashes of crimson, pink, orange, yellow and white among the peaceful greenery. What variety, intricacy, and splendour just in the plant kingdom!

The park with its gardens featured shady balustrades, gurgling fountains, and sparkling water pools amid tall trees, trimmed hedges, bright flowers, and neat lawns. Add chirping birds overhead, a friendly cat on the ground, friends chatting on a shady bench,

---

[16] Genesis 1:26-27; 2:7; 9:6; 11:6

children climbing the playground equipment – and the setting is reminiscent of paradise.[17]

Contrast to Divine Creation

By contrast, other human creations are far removed from the beauty of the Creator's handiwork. Ill-designed buildings in drab colours, graffiti disfigured walls, litter-filled streets, overflowing rubbish containers, noisy traffic, and polluted air offer little serenity and refreshment to the soul. Many suffer in dirt, deprivation and disease, together with tensions, quarrels, fighting, immorality and degeneration in environments largely devoid of anything edifying to the human spirit.

The two contrasting creations – one conducive to health and life, the other to sickness and death – can be analogous of the two distinctive trees said to have grown in the Garden of Eden. According to the Genesis narrative, the tree of life symbolized the way to eternal life and was freely available. The tree of the knowledge of good and evil signified a way of life contrary to the Creator and was forbidden. Although appearing good, it was deceptive, leading humans to suffering and death. The biblical record, not literal but nonetheless true, shows that humankind partook of the latter tree and has therefore acquired both

---

[17] Genesis 1:28-31; 2:8-9

kinds of knowledge – good and evil. This may help explain why humans are capable of stunning positive accomplishments as well as unbelievably evil deeds.[18]

Other Contrasting Creations

In a divine plan decreed in eternity, two other contrasting creations have been allowed to exist side by side – one old and one new. They are two states of the heart.

The first is the natural human heart, also referred to as a heart of stone – a hard, unbelieving heart, of and by itself unresponsive to God. Essentially deceitful, selfish, lawless, and blinded to the knowledge of God, it produces what the Bible refers to as the works of the flesh. These deeds include selfish ambition, idolatry, witchcraft, jealousy, envy, strife, rage, hatred, murder, immorality, debauchery and drunkenness. Other spiritual writers speak of a life ruled by the ego, focused only on the self. Inevitably the result includes the ugly creation described earlier with its accompanying pain and suffering.[19]

The Scriptures also speak of a new, pure heart. A gradual process of recreating the old heart is underway in some human lives. Through the power of the

---

[18] Genesis 2:9, 16-17; 3:1-8
[19] Jeremiah 17:9; Ezekiel 36:26-27; Romans 2:5; 8:5-7; Ephesians 4:18-19; Galatians 5:19-21

Holy Spirit, God is transforming the stony heart of people into a heart of flesh capable of understanding the things of God and pursuing a life of love and kindness. This new heart produces the fruit of goodness, joy, peace, patience, gentleness, faith, meekness and temperance.[20]

The Bible predicts a time when the being fuelling the old deceitful heart – who is described as the god of this world and ruler of the kingdom of the air; who instigates disobedience, hate and fighting; who is the father of lies and deception; whose aim is to steal, kill, devour and destroy – will be forever banished from influencing humankind.[21]

Ultimately, a new creation will shine forth – a new heaven and new earth, where sin, sorrow, crying and death will no longer exist or be remembered. Love, joy, beauty and peace will prevail forever.[22]

With the eyes of faith, we can catch glimpses of the new creation already today. However its full grandeur is yet ahead – a time when the people of God will be clothed with immortal, glorified bodies and will have unlocked for them all the mysteries of life they have

---

[20] 2 Corinthians 3:3; 5:17; 2 Timothy 2:22; 1 Peter 1:22; Galatians 5:22-23; 6:15
[21] 2 Corinthians 4:4; Ephesians 2:2; John 8:44; 10:10; 1 Peter 5:8; 1 John 3:8-10; Revelation 12:4-9; 20:2, 10
[22] Isaiah 65:17; 66:22; 2 Peter 3:13; Revelation 21:1-7

ever wondered about. This is the glorious hope of the ages beyond the sufferings of this life.[23]

---

[23] Romans 8:18-25; 1 Corinthians 13:8-12; 15:51-54

Life's Paradoxes and Mysteries

Mother Theresa and her assistants have devoted decades of their lives to selflessly serving the poorest of the poor in India. Friedrich Handel composed a magnificent oratorio, *The Messiah*, about the life of Christ. Michelangelo's Sistine Chapel paintings are a breathtaking work of art. Many others have greatly contributed to the relief of suffering, edification, and inspiration of fellow humans.

By contrast, for seemingly no reason or for their own selfish ambitions, individuals murder or attack others without provocation, damage property, or devise ways to cause harm. Cruel wars have killed billions over the course of human history – many accidentally. Countless others have been maimed physically, mentally and emotionally, as well as deprived of life's necessities in the demolition of basic infrastructure. Worse yet, ceasefires have often not ended the death and destruction with thousands of unexploded mines callously left behind to devastate innocent lives in future generations.

World of Paradoxes

Life on earth is full of opposites, paradoxes and mysteries. People can devote themselves in sacrificial love to the noblest causes. They can produce inspirational works of art, music or literature. On the other hand, they can dedicate their lives to causing destruction and death. Sometimes in the name of eliminating violence and establishing peace, more violence and devastation is brought about with far-reaching consequences.

The world promotes true and false values, good and evil, truth and misinformation. Beauty and ugliness, love and hate, health and sickness, life and death all co-exist. One cannot help but wonder: Why is that so? If there is a God and he is love, why do tragic things happen to good people? Why do the innocent suffer? Why are there wars with catastrophic consequences for billions? What about natural disasters, such as earthquakes, hurricanes, and tsunamis? Why do some people live in great abundance while others suffer extreme poverty and depravity?

The Scriptures also present many teachings that are paradoxical and incomprehensible to human logic. Among these are human free will operating in the context of divine sovereignty; Jesus Christ's earthly existence being fully human and fully divine; those having the indwelling Holy Spirit being guaranteed salvation, but exhorted to work out their own salvation and warned not to fall away from the faith; and God being one in three entities. Full answers to these and other questions are among life's mysteries and cannot be humanly fathomed. Nevertheless, the Bible provides some clues and a hope.

Possible Answers

Besides the sovereign Creator God, the Scriptures speak of another powerful being invisibly influencing events on earth – Satan the devil. While the biblical details of his origin are sketchy, he may have initially been a prominent, virtuous created spirit being under the name of Lucifer. According to some interpretations, pride and discontent led him to rebel against his Creator and thereby become God's adversary (together with other spirit beings, now demons). He is described as a liar, deceiver, murderer and destroyer.[24]

According to the biblical record of humanity – not a literal, historical account, but true nonetheless – Satan deceived the first humans to rebel against

---

[24] Isaiah 14:12-17; Ezekiel 28:12-17; John 8:44; 1 Peter 5:8; 2 Peter 2:4; Jude 6; Revelation 12:9

divine instructions. Consequently, the whole creation was subjected to futility and is in bondage to decay and death. Also as a result, human hearts became generally unreceptive to God.

The sovereign God has allowed Satan to exercise considerable, yet limited power over the world during the present stage of its history, and to influence and deceive humanity. However, we have also been given freedom of choice and a measure of authority over the created world. God calls individuals to be reconciled to him and to learn to discern between the true and false, the good and evil, the edifying and destructive. We are encouraged to pursue lives of kindness, peace, and service to others.[25]

Other factors that affect human hearts, minds, spirits and bodies are heredity, environment, lifestyle, and family background. (Some would add the consequences of behaviour in past lives.) Pain and suffering can be the result of poor judgment, violating divine or human laws, or God's discipline in a person's life for their ultimate good. Some suffering in this life appears to have no discernible causes. However, somehow God is present in all things – including disasters, crises and traumas – and works through them to accomplish his purposes for his glory and our ultimate good. Positive aspects of pro-

---

[25] 2 Corinthians 5:19-20; Ephesians 4:22-25

blems and difficulties are that we develop perseverance and maturity as well as understanding and compassion for others.[26]

Future Hope

Notwithstanding humanity's present condition, there is a promise and hope of ultimate deliverance and restoration of all things.[27] The Creator is actively and sovereignly involved in history. He predicts events in advance and brings them to pass. Mysteriously, he works within the bounds of free will that he gives to both Satan and humans. Acting quietly behind the scenes, God is pushing back Satan's dominion and implementing a plan of salvation decreed in eternity past and destined for fulfilment.

In reality, there is no battle between God and Satan where the outcome is uncertain. Rather, through the dramatic events surrounding the cross of Christ, Satan and his hordes are defeated foes, though not yet removed and still able to influence the minds and hearts of people.[28]

A time is indeed coming when a new heaven and new earth will be established without Satan's influ-

---

[26] Ephesians 2:1-8; 6:12-18; Galatians 6:7-9; Romans 1:28-2:10; 8:28; Hebrews 12:4-11; John 9:2-3; James 1:2-4
[27] 2 Corinthians 4:3-4; Ephesians 6:12; Job 1:6-12; 2:1-6; 1 Corinthians 2:11-14; Genesis 1:28; 2:16-17; 3:7-19; Romans 8:18-23; Acts 3:21
[28] Isaiah 46:9-11; John 12:31; Colossians 2:15; Romans 8:36-39

ence – with no sickness, suffering and death. The divine kingdom will rule the world and God himself will dwell among glorified humans. No longer will a mixture of good and evil, happiness and sorrow, and health and illness prevail, but only love, joy, peace and goodness. The whole creation will be liberated from its decay and changed to one of everlasting beauty and harmony.

While we may puzzle over many of the paradoxes today, including the origin of evil, we can eagerly anticipate a new world, where all of life's paradoxes and mysteries will be finally solved. Today, we only know in part, but when the divine promises of salvation are fulfilled, we will understand fully. What a fantastic hope and assurance! [29]

---

[29] Isaiah 11:6-9; 35:1-6; Revelation 21:1-5; Romans 11:33-34; Job 5:9; Ecclesiastes 8:16-17; 1 Corinthians 13:8-12; 1 John 3:2

Life and Death

A developing country grappling with modernity, Papua-New Guinea has infant mortality about 14 times higher than a developed country like Australia. Tragically, many babies and young children die before the age of five from preventable illnesses and are then abandoned by their parents. In Port Moresby, they are brought to the city morgue, where a social worker visits three or four times a year and arranges for their dignified burial outside the city. She gives each child a name, places the body in a tiny coffin, and keeps records of the burial locations in case any relative asks in the future.[30]

Perhaps only a few days ago the magpie in the park was flying from tree to tree, begging passersby for morsels of food. Now it lay lifeless on the wet

---

[30] The source of this story is ABC TV / Foreign Correspondent, Papua-New Guinea's Babies, aired March 4, 2008; http://www.abc.net.au/foreign/

ground. Its feathered body was intact, but its life was gone. It made me reflect on life as something truly miraculous. Humans, while able to boast breathtaking achievements, have not managed to create life in its truest sense. Sadly, sometimes life – human as well as that of other creatures – has been recklessly destroyed without regard for the consequences. What is life, anyway?

Some time ago, Ali, my nine-year-old Kuwaiti student, and I talked about the difference between living and non-living things. According to his textbook, all living things (other than plants) move, eat, grow and reproduce. The same is true of plants, except they remain in one place. Life makes creatures active and dynamic; death causes all activity to cease.

Life involves a constant flow of energy that keeps the necessary processes going. Many of them go on without much or any effort, or even consciousness, on the part of the living creature. As an oversimplified analogy, life is like a clock running on a battery. As long as the battery is charged, all the little wheels in the clock mechanism move and the hands show the correct time, day after day. When the battery is low, the clock may lose time, and finally it will stop.

The dead magpie will never fly again. Over a period of time, its colours will fade and through the work of ants and microscopic decomposers, its body will disintegrate. Its cells and molecules will be recycled and become parts of other organisms. The fate of a deceased person is much the same – no more movement, thoughts, feelings or plans. In a number of decades, only a few bones will remain. A sobering thought. Yet there is a difference between humans and other creatures. All humans – including the babies of Papua-New Guinea – have a hope.[31]

The Marvel of Life

Despite great advances in science, life (including the process of growth and aging) is not fully understood. It is a wonder that creatures of astonishing complexity develop from the fusion of two cells, each cell from a different organism, which then multiply by division. Even a single living cell is staggering in its intricacy. Its programming immeasurably supersedes that of the most sophisticated computer. Replicating itself over and over, its blueprint will differentiate into numerous body parts, each perfectly equipped for its role. At every stage of its development, each organ will "know" which direction to take and what to do.

When an organism has been fully formed, the energy that brought it about will drive each part to tirelessly function for the duration of its life. Instant

---

[31] Ecclesiastes 9:5-6, 10; Psalm 6:5; 115:17-18; 146:3-4; Isaiah 38:18-19

communication occurs between parts of the body as needs arise, and everything works in harmony. The creature itself is internally and unconsciously programmed with remarkable instincts and reflexes to do what it is supposed to and when. There are also degrees of intelligence – one could say that a mind is at work throughout the living world.[32]

In addition, everything in nature is interconnected and interdependent. The billions of living things ranging from microscopic unicellular organisms such as bacteria and viruses to giant mammals, and including among others, the vast plant and fungi kingdoms, all interact harmoniously. Overall, law and order operate throughout the creation – encompassing also the inanimate dimensions, such as seas, mountains, sun, moon and stars, as well as weather and climate.

Humanity in the Web of Life

According to the biblical creation story (which is not a literal history of origins, but nonetheless true), humankind is unique and was given responsibility to manage the rest of the natural world.[33] While greed, exploitation and short-sightedness have negatively impacted the environment throughout human his-

---

[32] See Gerald L. Schroeder, *God According to God*, Ch. 4, HarperCollins Publishing, New York, 2009.
[33] Genesis 1:26-29

tory, only in the last few generations has the intended harmony in nature been seriously disrupted.

Increasing worldwide industrial activity is contributing to global climate change with unwanted, destructive consequences, such as floods, droughts, hurricanes, and unseasonal weather patterns. Sex-selective population control is causing too many boys to be born and unbalancing the male-female ratio in the most populous nations. Medical science, while improving and prolonging human life as well as controlling some of the global health problems, has also inadvertently brought about the rise of drug-resistant bacteria and viruses, creating a threat of future worldwide deadly epidemics. Because the delicate natural balance has become significantly altered, many species are dying out.[34]

The present system of economics which promotes unlimited growth is in the long run unsustainable for the planet. Scientists and ecologists worry not only about depletion of non-renewable resources like oil and metals, but also about the overuse of renewable resources such as fish and forests, which are not allowed time to regenerate. Unless drastic changes are made in the economies and lifestyles of the affluent regions of the world, there is a danger of

---

[34] See Revelation 11:18

global lack of basic needs like food and water, without which life cannot go on.

Ultimate Life and Death

Scientists now believe that energy exists in all things, including the inanimate, and that some form of instant "communication" occurs at even sub-atomic and cosmic levels. Interestingly, Scriptures reveal that the Holy Spirit, the source and sustainer of life and the spirit of power or energy, totally fills the universe. Nowhere is the Spirit absent. Also, the apostle Paul taught the Athenians two millennia ago that we are in a way surrounded by God – in him we live, move and have our being and he is not far from any of us. Could this energy that scientists perceive as invisibly pervading all things, directing and upholding them until their appointed time is up, be an aspect of the sustaining divine Spirit? Further, according to the Bible, the Creator is aware of every sparrow that dies, and sustains and clothes every flower, not to mention the apex of creation, human beings who bear the divine image.[35]

In addition to physical life, the Scriptures also refer to another type of life – real life in contrast to the familiar relatively short life which ends in death

---

[35] Psalm 139:7-16; Acts 17:24-29; Matthew 6:25-34; 10:29-31; Luke 12:6-7, 24-31

100 percent of the time. To those willing to be reconciled with God the Father, Jesus Christ promised eternal life, the seed of which is already planted in this life. There is a promise of a future resurrection after a temporary cessation of this life. Death is symbolically portrayed as sleep or unconsciousness. Those who died having the Holy Spirit – the seed of eternal life – will wake up with a new glorious body when Jesus Christ returns to the earth. Instead of the corruptible flesh and blood body, as wonderfully made as it is, they will be given an incorruptible body that will never get sick, decay or die.[36]

In contrast with eternal life, the Word of God also speaks about eternal death – a death from which there will never be a resurrection to a future life. Referred to as the "second death", it will be accomplished through a "lake of fire". Christians in general, based on a few metaphorical verses, view the second death as eternal torment in hell. However, the teaching of a minority that those who reject the divine offer of life and grace will be forever destroyed may be closer to the truth. This idea of eternal death as opposed to eternal torment better corresponds to what the Bible reveals about God's nature, eternal life, and the incorrigible. If God personifies love and mercy and freely offers to humanity eternal life – in

---

[36] John 11:11-14; Romans 8:10-11; 1 Corinthians 15:51-57; 1 Thessalonians 4:13-17

contrast to eternal death, rather than eternal life in agony – it seems unlikely that the Creator will forever torture those who choose not to accept his offer of life. Whatever the exact details however, the fate of the wicked in terms of an ultimate or second death remains certain.[37]

To survive in our present existence, we need to be actively engaged in the four processes that characterize life. First, we must eat so that our bodies can produce body-building materials and energy that enable physical activity and renewal. Drink is needed to replenish lost water and to keep the body internally clean. Secondly, we have to be active – otherwise our organs will atrophy and stop functioning. Third, growth is necessary as when we stop growing, we degenerate. Finally, to enable the survival of the species in view of universal death, we must reproduce and replace ourselves.

The four life-sustaining processes also have spiritual parallels. Food and drink are required in the spiritual dimension of our lives. Through the Lord's Supper (referred to as the Eucharist by those of Catholic background), we partake of Christ's body and blood. Jesus who said that "man shall not live by bread alone but by every word that proceeds from the mouth of God" also refers to himself as the bread of

---

[37] Ezekiel 18:4, 20; Romans 6:23; Revelation 14:9-11; 20:10-15; Matthew 10:28; Psalm 37:9-10; Malachi 4:1-3

life. The written Word of God is compared to milk and solid food as well.[38]

Additionally, Jesus Christ, through the Holy Spirit imparts the water of life that permanently quenches thirst. The Holy Spirit is compared to living waters issuing from a converted person for others to be refreshed by. Through continued spiritual nourishment and faith, we build a closer relationship with God.[39]

Spiritually alive people grow in grace and love and in the knowledge of Jesus Christ. Looking to Jesus as their example and responding to the Holy Spirit within, they gradually take on Christ's likeness. In developing the mind of Christ, they are overcoming their selfish desires. Through the gift of divine grace, their lives bear the fruit of the Spirit, the greatest of which is love for God and love for fellow humans. Their example and teaching inspires others who then desire to learn more about their hope and lifestyle. In this way, new people are added to the spiritual body of Christ – the church, which grows as a result.[40]

---

[38] Matthew 26:26-28; 1 Corinthians 11:23-26; Matthew 4:4; John 6:35, 41; Hebrews 5:12-6:2
[39] John 4:10-14; 6:47-58; 7:37-39; 1 Peter 2:1-3
[40] John 14:15-20; Philippians 2:5-8; 2 Corinthians 3:18; Colossians 3:9-10; Galatians 5:22-24; 2 Peter 1:4-11; 3:18; Acts 2:22-41; 16:29-34

The Source of Life

In the natural world, only life begets life. Living creatures can only reproduce their own kind – through fertilized eggs or division. Using cloning, scientists can produce a genetically identical copy of a cell or living creature, but are unable to create life from scratch. None but the Creator God can bring life out of the non-living or dead state and sustain it.[41]

According to the creation account, the first humans, Adam and Eve, were created as clay figures and only came to life when given the "breath of life" (also referred to as "spirit of life"). The breath of life comes from God and returns to him upon death. It not only contains the life principle, but also seems to impart the mental, emotional and creative faculties (including reasoning, memory, will and imagination), as well as some spiritual comprehension, as seen in the many religions of the world. These God-given abilities separate humans from other creatures, as well as making each person unique.[42]

The Creator, as the one and only life-giver, has power over life and death. He both imparts life and takes it away at his discretion. However, he has given humanity a degree of choice between life and death –

---

[41] Psalm 104:27-30; Isaiah 42:5
[42] Genesis 2:7; Job 33:4; Ecclesiastes 12:7; Luke 23:46; Acts 7:59; 1 Corinthians 2:11-14

both at the physical and the eternal level. The way from death to life is only through a resurrection to another bodily existence (which can also be seen as a reincarnation or taking on another bodily existence), and the Bible alludes to more than one resurrection, over which God has total sovereignty.[43]

Adam and Eve initially had a choice between life and death. They had access to the tree of life, as well as a tree of knowledge, the partaking of which would result in death. Despite being instructed not to eat of the tree leading to death, they exercised their free will and imbibed of it. As an immediate consequence, their relationship with God changed from love to fear. With their connection to God disrupted, they, in a sense, died spiritually. They also lost access to the tree of life – representative of the Holy Spirit, the source of both spiritual and eternal life. Later they died physically and returned to the dust from which they came.[44]

As a result of their disobedience, their descendents were also barred from the tree of life and acquired the same, now sinful, ego-centred nature. And so down through the generations, all are born in a state that

---

[43] Deuteronomy 30:19-20; 32:39; 1 Samuel 2:6; Job 12:10; Matthew 10:28; John 11:25-26; 1 Corinthians 15:12-57
[44] Genesis 2:16-17; 3:1-24; 5:5

the Bible describes as "dead in sins" and are generally unreceptive to the things of God.[45]

Each of us is also given a choice – whether to invest the present life in divine purposes and reap eternal life or whether to pursue a life contrary to God's revealed way and experience the ultimate, or real, death. Physical death is certain. All people are destined to die – some after just a few short days, months or years; others after seven or more decades, or even a century. The awareness of death surrounds us daily – it meets us through the news and in our relationships with others. People are killed by bomb blasts, hurricanes, earthquakes, or in plane and car crashes. We hear of the famous dying of cancer or heart attacks. Close loved ones die of old age or a terminal disease. Nothing in this life is more certain than death. It is the inevitable result of our nature – the penalty of sin is death and this is an immutable law of the universe. The dead are cut off from God's life sustenance. However, for those who make the choice for God, there is a hope beyond death.[46]

Raised to Life

While we are all born spiritually dead – that is, unable of and by ourselves to gain access to eternal

---

[45] 1 Corinthians 1:18, 22-24; 2:6-14; Ephesians 2:1-5; Colossians 2:13-14
[46] Genesis 3:19; Romans 5:12; 6:23; Hebrews 9:27

life, God has not left humanity without recourse. Desiring all people to be saved, the Creator came to this earth in the person of Jesus Christ and through his own humiliating death enabled alienated humans to be reconciled with him. This is God's amazing offer of grace and pardon, which if accepted, opens the way from death to life.[47]

Although not all have accepted the offer of eternal life, many have yielded to God's drawing. In sorrow and contrition, they have perceived their hopeless condition and the need for a Saviour. They have responded to the Holy Spirit working in their hearts and minds, giving them a grasp of and yearning for spiritual things and active divine presence in their lives. At this point in their life's journey, like a fertilized egg, they have been begotten by God and received the seed of eternal life. Spiritually, they have been raised from death to life or born again, and figuratively have gained access to heavenly places.[48]

At Jesus Christ's second coming to the earth, those who have the indwelling Holy Spirit, and thus the germ of eternal life, will be either resurrected from their graves or, if they are still alive, be changed and given glorious new bodies. All those privileged to partake of this resurrection will never again be

---

[47] Ephesians 1:4-14; 1 Timothy 2:4
[48] John 1:11-13; 6:44; Romans 6:5-11; 1 Corinthians 1:21-24; 2:6-14; Ephesians 2:4-9; James 1:18; 1 Peter 1:3-5, 23

subject to death, disease, degeneration, pain and suffering – all the results of living in ways contrary to the Creator. Instead they will have a magnificent, joyful eternal future.[49]

Life and Death Struggle

We all know that life is not easy. In nature, there is a constant struggle for survival. Only the fastest, strongest and fittest survive. Human societies operate in a similar way – often the smart, ambitious, attractive, resilient and capable make it to the top. Sometimes, it is also the harsh and ruthless that become the rich and powerful.

Besides proven ways to reach success, such as goals, education, health, drive, perseverance and resourcefulness, other factors come into play for those who follow divine leading in their lives. Seeing the short-sightedness of striving for status, power and wealth, their vision of the future leads them to embrace the values of the heavenly kingdom of which they are already citizens. Their modus operandi is based on the way of love, kindness, humility and faith as they anticipate eternal life and immortality in the world to come. Because of their orientation, they

---

[49] Romans 8:9-11; Corinthians 15:22-26, 51-57; 1 Thessalonians 4:15-17; Revelation 21:3-5

often need to resist the world's values and may be ridiculed or persecuted for it.[50]

In addition to God's way being in conflict with the world's way, an internal struggle may also exist. Each person has two natures, though one may be inactive. People are born with human nature and inclined to seek independence from God. They also have a spiritual nature, which lies dormant. Alienated from the Creator, they are "dead in sins" and cut off from saving grace. (Of course, God is in all beings as the life-giver and sustainer, even if some may not acknowledge his existence.) When people are by grace spiritually enlivened and turn to God, the human and divine natures begin to work side by side. The Bible contrasts the "old man" – human nature, with the "new man" – the new creation in Christ.[51]

In a sense, a life and death struggle – a battle for our minds and hearts – exists between the human nature with its ego-driven inclination to selfishness and the divine nature imparted through the Holy Spirit. The human proclivity toward self-seeking, resulting in such things as imbalance, anger, hate and envy is at odds with the leading of the Spirit in the way of love, kindness and gentleness. Furthermore, as Satan tempted Christ to give in to the human lean-

---

[50] Romans 2:5-10; Galatians 5:19-25; 6:8-10; Ephesians 2:3; Philippians 3:20-21; 2 Timothy 3:12; 1 Peter 4:1-5
[51] Acts 17:28; Romans 8:5-8; Ephesians 2:4-9; 4:17-24

ings, he also tempts us to pursue pleasures, power and status.[52]

Jesus taught that a person needs to "lose their life for his sake" in order to preserve it for the kingdom. A sacrificial denial of one's ego, or the death of self, is called for. To pursue the upward call to holiness, we are instructed to put to death the ways of the sinful nature, to resist Satan, and to rise above the downward pulls of the world. The "old man" with its vices should be figuratively put off like a garment. As a new creation in Christ, we are to nurture the divine nature, bearing the "fruit of the Spirit" in our lives.[53]

As we continue our life journey in Christ, our mind and thinking are gradually transformed from within in such a way that the divine nature slowly replaces the self-dominated nature. The life and death struggle is being won through the power of the Holy Spirit inside – the mind is renewed, thoughts are brought into submission to Christ, and vices are replaced by virtues.[54]

While the miracle of physical life around us is something to marvel at, we can be even more awed by the miracle of human life being transformed into the

---

[52] Matthew 4:1-11; Romans 7:15-8:2; Galatians 5:16-18; Ephesians 6:12-13; 1 John 2:15-16

[53] Matthew 10:37-40; 16:24-25; Galatians 5:22-24; Colossians 3:5-14; James 4:4-7; 1 Peter 5:8-10

[54] 2 Peter 1:2-4; Romans 12:2; 2 Corinthians 4:16; 10:3-5; Galatians 2:20

divine image of Christ as the seed of eternal life within takes root and grows. And one day, we will see Jesus Christ as he is, and at that time fully take on his likeness, including immortality. This is the destiny of all who choose life over death, and being empowered by the Holy Spirit, gain victory in the life and death struggle.[55]

---

[55] 2 Corinthians 3:18; 1 John 3:2-3

Weather

Laughing kookaburras woke me at daybreak. Feeling rested, I got up and took my morning walk to the park. The white duck and the two brown ducks, hungry as usual, noticed me from afar and waddled towards me. My stopping by the pond to feed them quickly attracted other birds – swamp hens, turtle doves, ibises, mynas, and even a butcher bird or two. By this time, the sun's edge appeared above the horizon. The whole scene was inspiring – the rising sun, clear blue sky, cool summer breeze, chirping birds, and glistening water surface. It felt great to be alive – full of energy and motivated to go about the day's tasks.

A few days later, a cloudy morning sky greeted me outside. Rain didn't seem imminent, so I risked my walk without an umbrella. As I reached the pond, a shower came down, but luckily, I could wait it out under a picnic area shelter. I fed the birds, and when the rain stopped, continued my walk around the pond. The sun was now peeking out and the weather looked cheerier. As I reached the other side of the pond however, another shower came – this time heavier than the first one. With nowhere to hide, I walked on through it, arriving home dripping wet. Getting drenched that summer morning posed no big problem. Far worse would have been if it happened on the way to work or somewhere important.

Effects of Weather

Weather can inspire us, be unpleasant but tolerable, or cause significant problems. Its effects range from beneficial to frighteningly destructive. It affects our emotions and level of energy. With a gray sky and drizzle, the world outside looks dreary and inside lights may need to be switched on. A feeling of gloom, tiredness or lethargy may set in. While rain is vital for life, sometimes too much comes too fast. With heavy rain, water can quickly build up, causing flash floods that sweep away all that lies in their path.

A rain storm accompanied by fierce winds or large hail can break or uproot trees, bring down power lines, and damage buildings. A tornado roaring through an area may leave behind untold devastation. An electrical storm with its spectacular display of bright lightning and deafening thunder creates both awe and fear. Snow gives the countryside an impression of cleanliness, purity and peace, but excess snow produces havoc on roads and may cause roofs to cave in.

Weather and Life Seasons

The various weather patterns compare to seasons of life. Even language draws these parallels. Fine weather is like times when all is well – periods of productivity, contentment and peace. Gathering clouds picture times of potential trouble, and storms are times of crisis, when devastating losses may occur. On occasion, black clouds on the horizon pass by or disperse without a storm. Therefore, while responsible concern and prudence are good, excessive worry about possible problems tends to be unproductive.

Every life includes a share of both good and bad seasons. To hope for a life without problems and challenges is naive, just like it would be unrealistic to expect perfect weather all the time. Even in difficulties, however, one can always look for and be grateful for the good things, and anticipate that as in nature, each life storm will pass and the sun will shine again.

In some areas, the climate is such that weather itself causes many hardships. Parts of Asia, for example, are subject to severe annual flooding and the south-east coast of the United States and the Caribbean islands are subjected to one or more destructive hurricanes every year. By contrast, central and eastern Europe seldom experiences violent weather.

Just like some regions of the world get more severe weather than others, the number and type of storms in individual lives also varies. No one's life is problem free, but some people suffer more than others. The reasons may include unwise decisions, genetic factors, environmental factors, and more. Some would also add the consequences of what one did in a past life or lives.

Ultimately, all the reasons for why some suffer in indescribable ways, while others have relatively easy lives remain at this time part of the divine mystery. However, every trying situation is an opportunity for learning lessons, and growing in faith, patience, perseverance, determination, forgiveness, compassion, and other valuable character qualities.[56]

Biblical Weather Metaphors

The Scriptures use weather phenomena as analogies or metaphors for spiritual realities. Jesus Christ is referred to as the Sun of righteousness and his glorified face is said to shine as the sun in full strength. Like the sunshine on a cloudless day which

---

[56] 1 Thessalonians 3:2-4; 2 Thessalonians 1:3-7; James 1:2-4; 1 Peter 1:6-7; 4:12-18

gives us light and life-giving energy, God is the source of life, light and love. Through Jesus Christ, humans are empowered to live virtuous lives – they not only desire to obey God but have the power to overcome their undesirable traits and habits. God in his mercy, compassion and impartiality causes the sun to shine on both the just and the unjust.[57]

Rain in due season is a blessing. It brings refreshment on a hot day; provides life-giving water for flora and fauna; and is vital for food production. Lack of rain or unseasonal rain eventually leads to food shortages and famine. [58]

Rainstorms can symbolize times of testing. For instance, a series of setbacks and trials can beat on one's spiritual house, testing the strength of its foundation. In the Old Testament, a flood is also a symbol of judgment. The Bible relates a story of God having used a cataclysmic flood to destroy humankind after all had become corrupt. Only one just man, Noah, was spared with his family. Starting over again with one family and a few animals, God made a covenant with the earth that a widespread flood would never again devastate the world. The rainbow is a sign of that covenant.[59]

---

[57] Malachi 4:2; Revelation 1:13-16; John 8:12; 9:5; 11:25-26; 2 Corinthians 1:3-4; Matthew 5:45; 17:1-2
[58] Leviticus 26:3-4, 19-20
[59] Matthew 7:24-27; Genesis 6:13, 17-20; 8:21-22; 9:9-17

Based on the Scriptures, hail is also God's means of judgment. It constituted one of the ten plagues on Egypt before the Israelite exodus. Accompanied by thunder and lightning, the plague of hail caused terror and devastation. During their history, the Israelites also experienced discipline through hail when they refused to obey God. In the symbolic book of Revelation at the end of the Bible, hail is mentioned in futuristic prophecies as a part of severe plagues on the earth before the second coming of Jesus Christ. Hailstones of extraordinary weight and magnitude are described, which will terrify humans defiant against God. This period of unprecedented trouble prior to Christ's return is referred to as the day of the Lord, and is metaphorically characterized by darkness, clouds and gloominess.[60]

Weather and Humanity

Weather is a daily, hour by hour, minute by minute natural phenomenon. We experience it no matter where we are or what we do. There is no escape from it and little control over it. It affects our moods and feelings and is the subject of our conversations. Meteorologists can predict weather patterns and warn of violent weather before it happens. Never-

---

[60] Exodus 9:18-33; Psalm 78:48; Haggai 2:14-19; Revelation 8:7; 11:17; 16:21; Joel 2:1-3

theless, weather is determined by natural laws interacting in complex ways on the planet. Ultimately, weather and the laws governing it are under the control of higher powers.[61]

On the one hand, humans have no option but to adapt to the weather and learn lessons from it. On the other hand, some human choices influence the weather and climate. One of the great present concerns is how to halt the increasing effects of man-made pollution and global warming. Environmental experts and others are discussing the worldwide climate problems and realizing the interconnection and interdependence of all things. They are recognizing the need to safeguard the natural environment, to stop exploiting nature, and to practice responsible stewardship with future generations in mind. All agree that something needs to be done before it is too late. Some see that greed of a minority can no longer be allowed to motivate what is globally done with little regard for what effects it has on the other side of the planet.

While environmentalists are justifiably concerned and even worried about future human survival, the message of Scripture tells us that humankind will not destroy itself. Even though the Bible prophesies a time of unprecedented global trouble before Jesus

---

[61] Job 1:12,19; 38:22-30; Psalm 18:12-13; 78:47-48; 148:7-8; Ephesians 2:2

Christ's second coming, God also promises intervention and deliverance. Today, dark clouds are gathering on the horizon for a devastating worldwide storm in the end-time. However, the risen Christ is destined to save humans from self-destruction, renew the planet to historically unremembered beauty, as well as change human hearts and nature. Global destruction, wars and suffering will one day cease forever and a new bright age will dawn.[62]

---

[62] Matthew 24:21-31; Daniel 12:1-3; Matthew 19:28; Isaiah 2:2-5; 9:6-7; 11:6-9; 12:1-6; 25:6-9; Revelation 21:1-5

The Heavens and the Earth

Awed by seeing our beautiful blue planet as they were orbiting the moon, Apollo 8 astronauts were inspired to quote a part of the Bible passage below to people on the earth in a Christmas Eve telecast in 1968.

"In the beginning God created the heavens and the earth. ... And God said, 'Let there be an expanse between the waters to separate water from water.' ... God called the expanse 'sky.' And God said, 'Let the water under the sky be gathered to one place, and let dry ground appear.' And it was so. God called the dry ground 'land,' and the gathered waters he called 'seas.'...

"Then God said, 'Let the land produce vegetation: seed-bearing plants and trees on the land that bear fruit with seed in it, according to their various kinds.' And it was so....

"And God said, 'Let there be lights in the expanse of the sky to separate the day from the night, and let them serve as signs to mark seasons and days and years, and let them be lights in the expanse of the sky to give light on the earth.' And it was so. God made two great lights – the greater light to govern the day and the lesser light to govern the night. He also made the stars....

"And God said, 'Let the water teem with living creatures, and let birds fly above the earth across the expanse of the sky.'... 'Let the land produce living creatures according to their kinds: livestock, creatures that move along the ground, and wild animals, each according to its kind.' And it was so.

"Then God said, 'Let us make man in our image, in our likeness, and let them rule over the fish of the sea and the birds of the air, over the livestock, over all the earth, and over all the creatures that move along the ground.'"[63]

The biblical account of creation in Genesis 1 is not intended as a literal description of prehistoric origins. It is, however, supported by basic facts of science and some scientists have, upon closer examination, seen quite a few exact parallels.[64] The visible heaven is an

---

[63] Genesis 1:1-28
[64] See, for example, Gerald L. Schroeder, *The Science of God: The Convergence of Scientific and Biblical Wisdom*, Free Press, New York, 2009.

expanse above the earth where the sun, moon and stars are seen. The heavenly bodies separate day from night and determine the duration of months and years. Planet Earth consists of seas and dry land, both spheres teeming with plant and animal life suited to their environment. Humans are a unique form of life, ruling over the earth and the rest of the creatures, though as history and the present unfortunately show, not always responsibly. What lessons can be learned from the heavens, the seas and the dry land?

The Heavens

The atmosphere above the earth is the source of life-giving air. Without air, and especially oxygen which is essential for breathing, most life on earth would cease. Even thin air in high altitudes is challenging for mountain climbers as it has a negative effect on the body. Only organisms specifically adapted to the conditions can survive and thrive there.

Breath is a vital sign of life for land creatures and amphibians. (Fish also require oxygen for survival, but take it from the water through their gills, rather than from the air.) A person who stops breathing will soon die if not quickly resuscitated.

The Scriptures reveal that ultimately all life is given and sustained by God. Breath is also used as an analogy of the Holy Spirit. Without the indwelling Spirit, there is no spiritual life in the same way that without breath, there is no physical life. Those who have received the Spirit of God are promised a resurrection to eternal life after their death.[65]

The atmosphere also shields the earth's inhabitants from dangerous radiation. Damage to this protective layer, such as seen in the ozone hole above parts of the earth, has harmful consequences for humans and animals, including skin cancer and blindness.

The Bible refers to God as a protective shield for those who trust in him. Strong faith is a part of the "armour of God" – a shield against the darts of the evil one.[66]

From the sun, the earth receives light and heat, both of which are essential for life. Without them, the planet would be dark and frozen and plants couldn't produce vital oxygen through photosynthesis. The sun regulates the length of day and night, as well as the weather patterns of the seasons.

The Scriptures contrast light and darkness as symbols for goodness and the way of God on the one hand, and evil and the way of the devil on the other.

---

[65] Genesis 2:7; Job 27:2-4; 33:4; 34:14-15; John 20:22; Romans 8:10-11
[66] Deuteronomy 33:29; 2 Samuel 22:3, 31; Psalm 5:12; 28:7; Ephesians 6:11-16; 1 Peter 1:5

The two phenomena are also used as the contrast between truth and error, as well as between knowledge and ignorance. Light shows the way and truth sets people free. Darkness, by comparison, makes one stumble and sin enslaves people. Jesus Christ is metaphorically referred to as the Sun of righteousness and the Light of the world. His followers are to be a light to others.[67]

Air currents in the atmosphere, experienced as wind, are needed for water circulation between the seas and dry land. Without these streams of air no rain would fall and the continents would be all desert.

Wind in the Bible is used as another symbol of the Holy Spirit. As the effects of wind are seen but its precise working may not be clearly understood, the same is true about the Spirit. Wind brings life-giving rain to the earth. Similarly, the Holy Spirit is a source of spiritual and eternal life and is figuratively referred to as living water and being poured out.[68]

The Seas

At any time of the day, whether strolling along the beach, fishing from a boat, or riding the waves on a surf board, we cannot help but be impressed by the

---

[67] Malachi 4:2; Matthew 5:16; John 8:12, 31-32; 9:5; 11:9-10; Romans 13:12; 2 Corinthians 4:6; 1 Thessalonians 5:5
[68] John 3:8; 7:37-38; Ezekiel 34:26-27; 39:29; Joel 2:23-24, 28-32; Zechariah 10:1

ocean. Its vastness, restlessness, and hues mimicking the moods of the surrounding atmosphere reflect divine majesty. Bright sunshine from a cloudless sky gives the sea deep blue colour and a sparkle; full moon on a clear night makes it look silvery. The sea teems with life ranging from tiny plankton to gigantic whales. With the tides predictably governed by the gravitational pulls of the moon and sun, seas are full of energy. This cyclic rise and fall of the water – influenced by the sun's and moon's position in relation to the earth, the atmospheric pressure, and the wind currents – can be compared to the pulse beat of the oceans.

Analogies can again be drawn for the Christian life. Rocky outcrops in the sea are continuously under the onslaught of waves. Over time, they are eroded and smoothed at their rough edges. Similarly, human lives are beaten and shaped by events and experiences as well as the influence of the Holy Spirit within. Gradually, selfishness is eroded and one becomes more compassionate and concerned for others. The Scriptures speak about being washed from sins by the Word and Spirit of God.[69]

While the sea is vast and awe-inspiring, the water therein is undrinkable. Paradoxically, stranded sailors can die of thirst in the middle of an ocean if their

---

[69] 1 Corinthians 6:11; Ephesians 5:25-27; Titus 3:5-7

drinking water runs out. In the Bible, the Holy Spirit and the truth are compared to fresh and living water. In a world still under the influence of Satan, falsehood and deception abound. The sacred writings, however, speak of a time when the earth will be full of the knowledge of God like the seas are full of water.[70]

The Dry Land

The dry land consists mainly of mineral particles. They create sandy beaches and deserts; produce soil able to support vegetation; and form rocks and mountains. Much of the dry land is covered with plants, such as grass, bushes, trees, and cultivated crops. Many animals depend on the vegetation for food. Others, higher up in the food chain, depend on the herbivores for their sustenance. Everything works together in harmony – if not upset by unwise human practices.

Soils can be fertile or infertile, and hence of varying productivity. Soil can also be the source of precious stones and metals such as gold, silver, diamonds and iron. Another valuable commodity is oil and its derivatives upon which modern industry and technology heavily rely. The Word of God uses

---

[70] Jeremiah 2:13; John 7:38-39; Revelation 22:1, 17; 12:9; 2 Corinthians 4:3-4; Isaiah 11:9

the analogy of soil quality in relation to people's spiritual growth and the fruitfulness of their lives.[71]

Mountains in the Scriptures are often places of special significance or divine manifestation. From Mount Sinai, God spoke the Ten Commandments. Mount Gerizim and Mount Ebal were mountains in the Promised Land from which blessings for obedience and curses for disobedience were recited. God through Elijah demonstrated his power on Mount Carmel. Jesus was transfigured and glorified on a mountain, appearing together with Moses and Elijah. He will return to the Mount of Olives in Jerusalem where he spent many moments with his twelve disciples during his physical life. View from a mountain inevitably provides one with a fresh perspective on life.[72]

Built-In Adversity

When nature is rightly balanced, everything works together in harmony. However, struggle and adversity are built into the life cycles of many organisms. For example, migrating birds and butterflies face great odds on their journeys, struggling against rain, wind, exhaustion and hunger. Salmon start a new

---

[71] Matthew 13:3-8
[72] Exodus 19:16-25; 20:1-21; Deuteronomy 11:26-32; 27:11-14; 1 Kings 18:16-40; Matthew 17:1-7; 24:3; Luke 22:39; Zechariah 14:1-4

generation at the end of their lives by swimming upstream against incredible obstacles, to the place up the river where they hatched. Forest or steppe inhabitants must sometimes flee from fires, arctic creatures battle blizzards and extreme coldness, and desert animals are exposed to intense heat and dust storms. Nonetheless, even negative situations in nature can have an overall positive effect, such as fires clearing away dead matter and prompting new life to burst forth. Volcanic explosions, while potentially destructive, give rise to rich fertile soil.

Similarly in human life, God can and does work in adverse situations. Just as parts of the natural world are harsh and inhospitable and yet well-adapted life not only survives but thrives there, the same is true of human societies. Those in well-to-do western countries are often amazed at the hardship and suffering that people in developing nations are able to withstand.

Sometimes God allows, or may even bring about, adversity for humanly incomprehensible reasons. As Christians, we are called to resist surrounding evil influences even at the cost of personal suffering. Yet, while going through difficulties, we can be confident that God is there with us in the hour of trial. Ironically, divine presence is often seen much more clearly in adverse conditions than when all is going well. The Scriptures reassure us that in the long run, all things work together for good for those who love God and are called according to his purpose.[73]

Moreover, prophecies talk about a new heaven and new earth, where struggles, suffering, and even death will be things of the past. Humans will live in peace, children will be safe, and even wild animals will lose their ferocious natures. We don't know how this may come to pass or even to what degree it is literal rather than metaphorical. Either way, however, we can hope for and look forward to a new and better world, where God will live with people and all will experience unsurpassed love, beauty, and abundant life.[74]

---

[73] John 9:2-3; 2 Timothy 3:12; Hebrews 2:18; 4:15; 13:5-6; Romans 8:28
[74] Isaiah 2:2-4; 11:6-9; 65:17-25; Revelation 21:1-7; 22:1-5

The Marvel of Water

The summer temperature in Riyadh, Saudi Arabia, can approach 50 degrees Centigrade, though fortunately the heat is dry and therefore more tolerable than heat combined with high humidity. Nonetheless, whenever I needed to go outside during the day, I carried a small spray bottle with water. Squirting just a few drops in the form of water mist on my face and neck was very refreshing and made the extreme heat bearable. A cool drink of water on a hot day can similarly revive a wilted spirit as can a dip in a pool, river or the sea.

This precious resource is all around us. Water is such a part of our lives that we may take it for granted – till we experience a lack of it, or till it gets out of control. It covers two-thirds of the earth as oceans. It flows through streams and rivers, and gathers in ponds, lakes and seas. It is in the atmosphere, falls from the sky as rain, snow or hail, and condenses on the ground as dew. We drink it, wash in it, and swim in it. Without it we will die within a few days. Droughts bring crop failures and famines. Floods cause destruction, disease and death.

After hydrogen, water is the most common molecule in the universe. Outside the Earth, it exists as widely dispersed gaseous molecules and as formless, microscopic grains of ice. It also comprises a significant part of asteroids, comets, and planets. However, to exist as a life-giving liquid, it needs the precise conditions which as far as it is known exist only on our planet. This seemingly ordinary colourless, odourless and tasteless fluid is the simplest compound of the two most reactive elements in the universe, consisting of just two hydrogen atoms attached to a single oxygen atom. Despite its small size and simplicity, water is an extraordinary substance.

Unique and Indispensible

Liquid water is an absolute requirement and indispensable nutrient for life. We cannot live without it for more than about 100 hours, whereas other nutrients may be neglected for weeks or months. No other nutrient is needed in as great amounts and no substance constitutes a greater part of our bodies. The body water content varies among individuals, dropping with age, but averages about 90% of total weight for a foetus, 74% for an infant, 60% for a child, 57% for a teenager, 55% for an adult, and 52% for a senior citizen. Male bodies contain a little more water than those of females due to a difference in the amount of fat. A balance needs to be maintained between water intake and loss.

Without water life cannot start or continue. Water plays vital roles within the body. It acts as a medium for and a contributor to, molecular interactions, and as a reactant in many metabolic processes. No enzymes can work in the absence of water molecules. The polarity and small size of the molecules make water an excellent solvent. As such, it carries and distributes nutrients, hormones, and other materials around the body and within cells. It assists in waste removal, mainly via the urine and faeces. It is a lubricant between bodily structures, such as joints. It also acts as a shock absorber, for example for the brain or for the unborn child.

It is water's unique properties and its ability to change to suit the circumstances that so perfectly meet the requirements for life. Intriguingly, liquid water acts in subtly different ways as conditions change, responding to variations in the physical and molecular environments, and occasionally acting as though it was present in more than one liquid phase. In other words, sometimes liquid water is free-flowing while at other times, in other places, or under subtly different circumstances, it acts more like a weak gel. No other liquid can replace water as no other molecule comes close to having its remarkable properties.

The large heat capacity and high thermal conductivity of water, together with the high water content in organisms, contribute to thermal regulation and small temperature fluctuations. As a result, living organisms can successfully maintain their body temperature. The high latent heat of evaporation gives resistance to dehydration and provides cooling.

At four degrees Centigrade, water expands on both heating and cooling. This means that ice has lower density than water, and freezing cannot occur before the temperature of the whole water body is close to four degrees Centigrade. As a result rivers, lakes and seas freeze from the top down. This permits survival of life at the bottom, insulates the water from further freezing, and allows rapid thawing.

The large heat capacity of the oceans and seas allows them to act as heat reservoirs. Hence sea temperatures vary only a third as much as land temperatures and moderate the global climate. For example, the Gulf Stream carries tropical warmth to north-western Europe.

The compressibility of water reduces the sea level by about 40 metres, allowing for five percent more land. Water's high surface tension, together with its expansion on freezing, encourages rock erosion which provides soil for agriculture.

The unique properties of water required for life-giving processes result from the specific strength of the hydrogen bonds in the molecules and molecule clusters. If the hydrogen bonds were stronger, water would behave like glass. Weaker bonds would cause water to exist as a gas and only become a liquid at sub-zero temperatures. Even very slight strengthening or weakening of the hydrogen bonds would significantly change the metabolism of living organisms. For example, DNA would not form helices that are able to zip and unzip, and enzymes would not possess a three-dimensional structure or retain the controlled flexibility required for their biological action.

Holy Spirit – the Living Water

The New Testament uses water as a symbol of the Holy Spirit, metaphorically referred to as living water.[75] Indeed, water has many properties that can somewhat help us understand the qualities of the all-pervasive divine power and energy.

---

[75] John 4:10-14; 7:38-39

No other substance is commonly found in all three states – as solid, liquid and gas. This three-in-one existence can give us a glimpse into the nature of the Trinity comprising God the Father, Jesus Christ, and the Holy Spirit. We can to a small degree imagine how there is one God, but three entities in the Godhead.[76]

Physicists believe that water molecules can be found throughout the universe. However, as far as we know, only the Earth has enough life-supporting liquid water. In a similar manner, the biblical psalmist affirms that the Holy Spirit is omnipresent – there is nowhere in the cosmos that one can escape from the Divine.[77] However, as water appears to play a unique life-giving role on our planet, the Scriptures suggest that it is on Earth, in human beings, that the Spirit is working in a special way in the drama of salvation.[78]

Water is an indispensable agent in starting and maintaining the processes of life, fulfilling hundreds of functions. Without water, seeds will not germinate and seedlings will not grow. Life soon comes to an

---

[76] Matthew 28:19; Acts 2:32-33; Romans 15:15-19; 2 Corinthians 13:14; Titus 3:4-6; Hebrews 9:11-14
[77] Psalm 139:7-16. Interestingly, scientists have detected forms of universal, yet incomprehensible, energy without which the physical world would cease to exist. So called "dark energy", which accounts for 73% of the total mass–energy of the universe, is a hypothetical form of energy that permeates all space and tends to accelerate the expansion of the universe.
[78] Psalm 8:3-9; 144:3-4; Hebrews 2:6-11

end. In a similar way, all that exists would cease to do so if not sustained by spirit energy. According to the Genesis account (which although not intended to offer a scientific explanation of origins contains inspired truth), the Holy Spirit was present at creation and instrumental in the origin of life. The Bible indicates that the Spirit also maintains the innumerable life processes and physical laws, so that they continue functioning.[79]

Besides sustaining the brief physical life, the Holy Spirit also imparts eternal life or ultimate immortality to humans. Without it, death and decomposition occur in just a few short decades, without hope for any hereafter. The inspired Word documents several instances of where the physical life of people was prolonged through a resurrection from the dead. However, only Jesus Christ permanently conquered death by passing from physical death onto eternal life. At his return to the earth, those who have the Holy Spirit working in them are promised the same type of resurrection to eternal life.[80]

Water enlivens what appears dead. Seemingly lifeless desert landscapes miraculously spring to life with just a little rain. Likewise, the Holy Spirit enlivens those who are spiritually dead, enabling them to re-

---

[79] Genesis 1:1-2; Job 12:10; 33:4; Psalm 104:10-30; Nehemiah 9:6
[80] Romans 8:9-11; John 11:11-14, 38-44; Acts 9:36-41; 1 Corinthians 15:20-23, 51-54

spond to the divine calling and other spiritual realities. When our ancestors disobeyed God's instructions, the offer of eternal life was withdrawn and they died spiritually. Their nature changed, and they and their descendants were from then on to experience only a temporary physical life and physical realities. God, however, continues to reach out to humanity with special grace. Those who are able to respond become "born from above" through the "spirit of life". When that happens, a new spiritual life springs forth, working a transformation of mind and heart.[81]

Nothing can substitute for water in the life-sustaining processes – it is a unique and irreplaceable substance. Similarly, the Holy Spirit is the only way to eternal life and salvation – this special gift provides a guarantee of a future resurrection.[82]

As water performs multiple functions in the physical body, enabling it to grow and develop, so the Holy Spirit plays many roles in the spiritual body of Christ, the church, and is instrumental in its growth. One of its functions appears to be that of an executor. Through a virgin conception, the Spirit merged divinity (the Son of God) with humanity (the Son of Man). At Pentecost, the Spirit empowered the disciples to do even greater works than the God-man

---

[81] Genesis 2:16-17, 3:1-8, 22-24; Ephesians 2:1-13; John 3:3-8; 17:1-3; Romans 6:23; 8:1-2; 12:2; Titus 3:5-7
[82] John 6:44, 65; Acts 4:12; Romans 8:8-11

Jesus did while on earth. The Spirit draws individuals to God the Father, convicts them of sin and the need for a Saviour, and upon their response, brings them to conversion. He guides the operation of the church, equipping members with special gifts for the edification of all. The Spirit is a unifying power, leading people to the one body, one hope, one Lord, one faith, one baptism, one God and Father. He also places individuals in the body as it pleases him.[83]

Water transports nutrients, removes waste, and improves appearance. It lubricates joints for smooth, painless functioning, and serves as a reactant and catalyst. It also structures molecules to enable them to carry out their roles. The Spirit brings people into contact with the gospel and opens their hearts and minds, enabling them to understand the truth of salvation and respond to God. He cleanses the mind and heart from impure thoughts and motives and renews lives. The results are seen in expressions of love, patience, kindness, joy and peace. Furthermore, the Spirit lubricates relationships, smoothing over differences and producing unity and harmony. In addition, he is a sovereign and active participant in world events. Like a reactant and catalyst, having determined the timing and outcomes beforehand, he

---

[83] Matthew 1:18-20; John 14:12; Acts 2:1-4; 3:19; 16:6-10; 20:28; 1 Corinthians 12:7-18; Ephesians 4:3-7

brings about events, or speeds them along as necessary, to fulfil God's purposes.[84]

Few places exist where water cannot penetrate. As it runs over rocks and seeps into their crevices, it erodes them, smoothes them, and breaks them up, creating soil in the process. The Holy Spirit penetrates the crevices of the heart, breaks up the stony heart, and erodes the rough edges of the marred image of God. Depending on a person's responsiveness, the Spirit can create a fertile soil for the seed of God's Word and help bring about a spiritual harvest of the fruits of righteousness. As liquid water can modify its state depending on the environment and circumstances, so the Spirit works differently at various times, in diverse cultures, and in the lives of individuals.[85]

Water quenches thirst, cools, refreshes and revives, especially in the heat of the day. Comprising a large part of our bodies, it permeates cells and molecules, guiding their functions. The Spirit, as a personal helper, quenches spiritual thirst for the things of God, and assists believers in life's trials as a comforter, assuring them of God's love and adoption. He fills the hearts of believers, and as a guide, imparts

---

[84] Psalm 33:11; Ezekiel 12:25; John 17:22; 1 Corinthians 2:7-14; Galatians 5:22-23; Ephesians 5:25-27; Titus 3:4-7
[85] Matthew 13:13-23; 2 Corinthians 9:10

thoughts according to God's will and plan for our lives to shape our decisions and behaviour.[86]

Water stabilizes body temperature and moderates global climate. The Holy Spirit is a spirit of moderation and self-control in individual lives. Through those who exemplify the fruit of the Spirit and are lights of the world, the Spirit counteracts the spiritual darkness and evil that would otherwise be even more rampant.[87]

Water reflects what is above it, even at a distance. The Holy Spirit can be seen as reflecting the spiritual realities of heaven. He interprets for us the things of God so that we can better understand them and so leads us into a deeper appreciation of Jesus Christ and the plan of salvation. The Spirit opens to us biblical revelation as well as prompting inspiration and insights from nature and day-to-day experiences. He has also inspired writers and editors down through the centuries to record what we need to know for a life leading to eternity in glory.[88]

So the next time we walk through a meadow wet with dew, get caught in a rain shower, stroll along the seashore, swim in a lake, or drink a cool glass of

---

[86] John 14:16-18, 28; 16:7, 13; Romans 8:12-17; 26-27; Ephesians 2:10
[87] Matthew 5:14; Galatians 5:22-23; Ephesians 5:8-10; 2 Peter 1:5-8; 2 Timothy 1:6-7; 3:1-5
[88] Galatians 4:6-7; John 14:26; 15:26; Hebrews 3:7-14; 1 Timothy 4:1-2; 2 Timothy 3:16-17; 1 Peter 1:10-12

water, let's reflect on the amazing properties of both the physical and spiritual "water of life". Both are a marvellous gift and blessing from God.[89]

---

[89] Psalm 65:9-10; Ezekiel 34:25-27; John 4:10-14

Riverside Reflections

On an early summer day, the tour bus made its way to Rock Riverside Park. One of the largest in the Brisbane area, the park provides facilities for recreational activities for all ages. It has about 800 metres of frontage along the Brisbane River where visitors can take a walk, ride a bike, roller-skate, or enjoy barbeque lunch at a picnic table while watching boats and barges go by.

Continuing on to the Brisbane city centre, the scenic waterway offers other opportunities. Kayaking and canoeing are available both during daylight hours – past glass skyscrapers, historic buildings, and old wooden homes – and at night against the glittering city skyline of the lit-up city. Boat cruises traverse the river at regular intervals.

Stopping at the City Botanic Gardens on the river's north bank offers a chance for a peaceful, even meditative break, followed by a picnic lunch beneath mangroves and macadamia trees. The South Bank features alfresco cafes and dining places overlooking the river which cater to a wide variety of tastes and budgets.

Spending time by a river and watching it glide past the natural or man-made environment on its banks, glistening in the sun or reflecting the mood of the sky, can inspire reflections on the nature of the waterway and its surroundings, their parallels with life, as well as spiritual analogies. Here are some that come to mind.

Rivers and Their Environs

Every river has a tiny beginning at a mountain spring or a lake that has formed from rain or melting snow. Gradually, the small stream becomes a part of something greater as it merges with other streams along the way, and ultimately reaches its destination and empties into a lake, sea or ocean. A river is never the same – every moment is different in its continuing flow from source to destination. Heraclitus (c. 535 - c. 475 BCE) correctly observed that you never step into the same river twice.

Along its course and over time, a river is a "witness" to countless scenes and events in its path and on its banks. Upstream this may include groups of thrill-seeking rafters in their inflatable boats braving the choppy waters and dodging rocks. A little further down, several hungry bears may be impatiently waiting for the salmon run when thousands of fish swim upstream on their final journey to spawn in the same place where their lives began half a decade before that. Still further along the river's now peaceful flow, fertile fields, lush meadows with bright flowers, and tall trees swaying in the breeze may flank the banks, with distant hills or mountains on the horizon. Along the way, the stream will have merged with a number of tributaries and swelled in size.

Yet further downstream, several towns and cities with homes, office buildings, factories, recreational parks, and even churches and temples may straddle the river, now several hundred metres wide. People are crossing it over impressive bridges, some on foot, others in cars, buses, trains or trucks. Ships and boats of all shapes and sizes, some carrying passengers, others loaded with goods, can make the river appear almost as crowded as the six-lane bridge above it.

Along its course, the river flows over and around obstacles like rocks, smoothing them over time. It carries and redeposits fallen branches, leaves, sediments, and other debris. If pollutants have been poured into the water from an external source or solid rubbish thrown in, they too are carried downstream. Sometimes a river drops down sharply over a cliff, forming a spectacular waterfall – its spray creating a rainbow through the sun's rays.

The river supports and nourishes life within it – a whole range of aquatic plants and animals, including those of microscopic sizes, as well as creatures that feed on these. It also assists vegetation and wildlife on its banks. In addition, it provides water for drinking and other uses to humans, as well as power to industry. A river can move briskly, but also calmly and peacefully, glistening in the sun and providing refreshment and relaxation for people along its shores. At the other extreme, in one of its angry moods, it can become a raging torrent leaving destruction and death in its path. Yet, even though floods can be devastating, when a river floods and recedes, it leaves behind fine sediments like clay, mud and silt. These deposits create very fertile soil providing rich nutrients to plants. Because of these benefits, flood plains are prime real estate for farmers.

People have often tried to change rivers and riverbanks to suit their needs and even to satisfy their greed. Rivers have been dredged, dammed and rerouted. Riverbanks have also been denuded of trees and other vegetation. Waterways have been ignorantly or selfishly used as waste disposals – showing a gross lack of understanding or respect for the finely balanced natural ecosystems. Much of such human intervention has had negative environmental effects resulting in polluted, dying, or even disappearing rivers with drastic changes to habitats and their organisms. Originally clear waters have become murky with excessive concentrations of pesticides, fertilisers, and other undesirable substances, which cause suffering, sickness and premature death to fish and other aquatic life – and ultimately even move up the food chain to adversely affect humans.

Life as a River[90]

Many a river has inspired poets, playwrights, composers and artists. John Burns[91] referred to the Thames as "liquid history", a description that fits rivers universally. As a river flows, over time it witnesses events and history unfold both inside the riverbed and along its banks. It is interconnected with its environment as are the human lives in its vicinity interconnected with the river. In fact, ancient civilizations regarded rivers as sacred – a divine gift – and understood their physical and spiritual survival as dependent on the river.

Each of our lives can be seen as an individual river with its unique origin, journey and destination. Every person has his or her own history that they have

---

[90] For a number of the ideas in this section, I am indebted to the website http://www.helium.com.
[91] 1858-1943; English politician and expert on London history

written and continue to write along the way. As rivers vary in length, our lives do too. We each start like a tiny mountain spring or a small overflowing mountain lake. Regrettably, some don't get much past this humble beginning. Most of us, however, flow along on our journeys, but don't know where or how far our estuary or final destination is. As tributaries join a river, so our circle of friends and acquaintances expands beyond our immediate family.

Our experiences are like the scenes and events along the course of a river – both in the riverbed and along the banks. Just like every stretch of the river has a story to tell, so does every year, month, week, day, hour, and even each minute of our life. Like the flow of a river, life's experiences can change moment by moment – everything is impermanent and will sooner or later pass. That is why living in the present, valuing and being grateful for every special moment, is important, as compared to obsessing with either the past or future.

As the various river ecosystems – vegetation, wildlife, aquatic life, even human civilization – intertwine and influence each other, our lives are intertwined with the lives of others and our environment. Indeed, "no man is an island" as 17th century poet John Donne wrote in his *Meditations*. Also, quantum physics teaches us that we are all one in essence and our separateness is just an illusion. Therefore all our thoughts, words and actions influence others and vice versa. We can enrich other people's lives by receiving them, listening to them, and compassionately respecting them. We can also care for nature and other creatures and thereby positively affect the environment. On the other hand, like a polluted river, we can have a negative effect on those around us by mindlessly spreading toxic thoughts, words and emotions. Likewise, thoughtless actions can be destructive to our surroundings.

A river can flow calmly and peacefully, or briskly, even hurtling over a cliff. Our lives can feel the same – sometimes all is flowing smoothly, with only minor obstacles in our paths. By contrast, at other times, life's events can throw us around roughly, not unlike river rapids – we may feel as if cast into a raging torrent and sinking, or worse still, heading over a cliff. Whether the river of our life is tranquil or turbulent, any and all experiences on our journey can give us insights and teach us lessons – if our minds and hearts are open to them.

Often we are not able to control what happens, but our response and what we make of any particular situation is in our hands. Sometimes, we impulsively react rather than thoughtfully respond and then reap less than positive consequences, making an already unfavourable situation worse. Hopefully, of course, the next time we will have learned from the experience, gained wisdom and compassion, and will deal with a similar challenge better. As a river flows along its riverbed, generally unaffected by what is happening on its banks, we too need not react to others' thoughts, anger or ill will. Needless to say, learning can also come, often easier if we heed, from the experiences of others.

Each river follows a path from source to destination – it trusts the flow of its current and submits to it. Similarly, to mindfully follow the flow of our life can be the best and easiest way, in contrast to constant struggle fuelled by selfish desires and ambitions. In fact, the continuous desire for more money, power, possessions or status, and the resultant striving, is what keeps us dissatisfied, ungrateful and unhappy. Since God is both our source and destination, we need to keep checking along the way that we are following the path of divine will and guidance and fulfilling our God-given calling and purpose.[92]

A river is dependent on its source for its flow and life – it is renewed and restored by its spring, in addition to rain and tributaries along its way. Likewise, we are dependent on our divine source for survival and renewal. Additionally, our bodies have inherent restorative power within them. Finally, we are also nurtured by others along the way – be it family,

---

[92] Ecclesiastes 12:7; John 13:3; 16:28; Hebrews 2:6-15

friends, and sometimes even strangers who cross our path.[93]

Rivers are agents of change within themselves and to their environment. Life, too, will change us along its passage – as a result of our experiences, our personalities change, we learn lessons, acquire wisdom, and become kinder and more compassionate. In turn, we affect our environment and those around us. Hopefully our influence on our surroundings and fellow pilgrims on earth is more life-giving than destructive.

All rivers will directly or indirectly reach the ocean – which is where they started from as a part of the natural water cycle. It is evaporation from the sea that forms clouds, which when wind-driven over mountain peaks drop down water in the form of rain and snow. Some of this precipitation then gives rise to creeks and rivers, which in turn return to the ocean, thus completing the cycle. As mentioned, our lives have their origin in the immanent Divine – "in him we live and move and have our being".[94] Our spirit or "soul" came from God and will return to God. So in a way, as the river began in and returns to the ocean, at the end of our earthly journey, we'll return to and unite with our divine source.[95] Much on the

---

[93] Psalm 3:5; 41:3; 55:22; Hebrews 3:13; 10:25; Philemon 1:7
[94] Acts 17:28
[95] Ecclesiastes 12:7

physical plane, including the "life" of a river and our own lives here and now, remains a mystery – and this is even more so for life beyond the grave.

Spiritual Analogies of a River

Rivers and streams, as well as riverside places, figure prominently in the Scriptures – often as metaphors for life and blessings. Without water, life cannot exist for long and fertile areas soon turn into deserts. A tree by the river, in contrast, is green and rich in fruit. It is used as a metaphor for a virtuous person, one who, watered by the living water of the Holy Spirit (another metaphor), also blesses and refreshes those around by the fruits of love, peace, faith and kindness flowing from within.[96]

A cool path along a stream is a symbol of divine care and comfort. A land flowing with streams of water is a blessed land.[97] In the New Testament, a river was sometimes a place of baptism – the baptism symbolizing death of the old self and rising to a new life in God. The river bank was also a place of prayer.[98]

The old and the new Paradise are both associated with a river, fertile trees, and life. The symbolic Garden of Eden was watered by a river and grew trees of

---
[96] Psalm 1:3; John 7:37-39; Galatians 5:22-23
[97] Numbers 24:6; Deuteronomy 8:7; Psalm 23:1-2; Jeremiah 31:9
[98] Mark 1:5; Acts 16:13

all kinds, including the tree of life in the middle. The restored Paradise in the new heavens and earth is said to have the river of life flowing through it and multiple trees of life with a never-ending harvest on its banks.[99]

A riverside outing can provide not only recreation and rejuvenation, but upon reflection, also give glimpses into the higher realities of the "water of life" – the Holy Spirit. If the Spirit flows from within, as Jesus promised it would, then through our behaviour we can refresh those we interact with.[100] We can each become like a life-giving spring, a fountain offering a cool drink to quench thirst for love and acceptance. Or, like a tree, nourished by a stream, which provides shade from the scorching heat of anger and hate, or supplies luscious fruit to ease the gnawing pain of hunger for purpose and meaning. Each of us in this life will encounter and join with other "rivers" – potentially increasing our effectiveness. And hopefully along the length of our flow, we'll nourish and deposit good soil for the plants and trees along our banks, thereby helping to minimize the spreading of pollution and destruction.

---

[99] Genesis 2:10; Revelation 22:1-2
[100] John 4:14; 7:37-39

Springs in the Desert

On my flight from Bahrain to Riyadh, Saudi Arabia, I marvelled at the vast expanse of desert landscape below – no vegetation except for an isolated bush or tree; no rivers, fields or forests; nothing but emptiness mile after mile. The same held true on a later bus trip to the Al Quassim area west of Riyadh. Apart from occasional towns and ruins of historical buildings, the scenery consisted mostly of endless plains of dry sandy soil with scattered areas of barren scrub.

Riyadh is a sprawling city surrounded by the deserts of central Arabia. In the 1970s, most of the embassies moved from Jeddah to the Diplomatic Quarter of Riyadh. This area with its cultivated parks and gardens, as well as a wadi area with irrigated palm groves is like an oasis. The effect of water in the desert is miraculous – transforming a seemingly dead area into a living one.

Desert conditions result from extreme heat and lack of water. There are, however, degrees of barrenness. Even with minimal water, a desert is not lifeless. A few hardy plants survive and thrive. Tracks in the dust betray the presence of a variety of animal kinds – ants, beetles, caterpillars, lizards, hedgehogs and birds, among others. But life is not easy. A dead toad still sitting up, seemingly cooked in the scorching sun while hopping across the road, is a sobering sight.

The desert barrenness makes humans vulnerable. Without food and water in the intense daytime heat and harsh night-time coldness, a person cannot survive for long. It is easy to get disoriented and lose one's way in the monotonous terrain where everything looks the same. Furthermore, dust storms that drastically reduce visibility and rare torrential rains that turn the desert into a muddy swamp make journeying extra challenging. Many a traveller has met an untimely end in the desert.

Deserts in the Bible

Expanses of desert exist in the area where biblical history is set – the Middle East and North Africa. As a result, desert settings feature prominently in the Scriptures. They are spoken of as places of testing and manifestations of God, as well as areas of refuge or spiritual retreat.

Moses spent forty years in the desert after escaping from Egypt where his life was sought for murder. He married, had two sons, and lived with his father-in-law Jethro's family when God appeared to him and gave him the special task of bringing his people out of Egyptian slavery. So, starting at age 80, he spent another forty years in a desert wilderness as he led the people of God, Israel, to the Promised Land. [101]

King David and the prophet Elijah both escaped into the desert before pursuers who sought their lives.[102]

Later, just prior to the time of Christ, in the desert of Judea, John the Baptist preached Jesus' coming as the Messiah and exhorted to repentance.[103]

For forty days at the beginning of his ministry, Jesus was tested in the desert by being subjected to Satan's temptations. Later, he and his disciples retreated into the desert to get away from crowds.[104]

Life as a Desert Experience

On their desert journey, the Israelites suffered thirst, hunger and discouragement. Without God's

---

[101] Acts 7:27-38; Exodus 2:11-15; 3:1-10; Deuteronomy 1:30-33; 2:7; 32:10-18
[102] 1 Samuel 23:14-19; 26:1-4; 1 Kings 19:1-8
[103] Matthew 3:1-12; Mark 1:3-8
[104] Matthew 4:1-4; Mark 6:31; Luke 9:10

loving leadership, provision and sustenance, they would not have survived their forty-year odyssey.[105]

Human life can be compared to Israel's desert journey – many times it seems dry, difficult and disorienting. One may feel like wandering through a giant labyrinth, going in circles, or hitting dead ends. After at the most a few decades, conscious human existence comes to an end, with the physical body slowly disintegrating into dust where it came from. Yet all is not hopeless.

The Scriptures provide a clue to the origin of this earthly "desert experience". When our ancestors disregarded their Creator's instructions, they alienated themselves and their descendents from God. Nevertheless, in his faithfulness, God did not abandon humanity. A means of reconciliation has been made available as God, through Jesus Christ, took on human form and died for mankind. While the first people lost access to the tree of life, the way has again become open for those who choose life over death. They have an opportunity to respond to God's grace in faith and submission – as opposed to remaining separate and independent from God, which results in physical and spiritual death.[106]

---

[105] Deuteronomy 8:2-5, 15-16; Psalm 78:13-16, 20, 23-29, 52-55
[106] Genesis 2:16-17, 3:22-24; John 1:1-5; 9-13; 3:16-19; 1 Corinthians 15:45-49

While selfish human exploitation of the environment is causing present deserts to enlarge, the Bible gives hope for a future restoration of all things. The prophets spoke reassuringly to the Jewish people exiled in Babylon that one day they would again be restored in their own land. They also wrote of watered deserts springing into bloom. When even now with just a little rain, seemingly lifeless seeds in the ground germinate overnight and a barren area suddenly becomes carpeted in green, how much more will running springs of water accomplish! One can only imagine today's inhospitable deserts having their thirst quenched by gushing water forming pools and lakes, and turning the wasteland into a paradise-like garden.[107]

Spiritual Parallels

For the people of God today, the prophecies of deserts blooming have a powerful application to life in the Spirit. The hope for the deserts remains a hope for humanity. Of and by themselves, separate from God, humans in this life can be seen as spiritually dead, and after a relatively short bodily existence will also die physically. Through the Creator's amazing grace, however, the Holy Spirit – symbolized as living

---

[107] Isaiah 35:1-2, 6-7; 49:8-10; 51:1-3; Ezekiel 36:32-38

water – has a transforming power both in the physical life and after death.[108]

Touched by the divine Spirit, a lifeless, depressing and meaningless existence will begin to reflect love, joy, peace and hope. The Spirit is like a seed of eternal life implanted within a person. When Jesus returns to the earth as a king over the kingdom of God, those who died in Christ, lying in the ground like dormant seeds, will come to life and no longer be subject to death. They will undergo an incredible transformation from mortal to immortal, from corruptible to incorruptible.[109]

The Word of God holds out a cosmological hope for humanity that is incomprehensible in its scope and magnificence. Ultimately, humans will be fully restored into the divine image for which they were destined and all things will be made new. A just and righteous rule of the kingdom of God will become universal. There will be no more suffering and death. All will know God, and the new heavens and earth will be filled with love and gladness throughout eternity.[110]

---

[108] Ephesians 2:1-8; John 4:10-14, 7:37-39
[109] Isaiah 32:15-20; Galatians 5:22-23; Romans 8:6-11; 1 Corinthians 15:51-54
[110] Isaiah 11:9; 43:19-21; Zechariah 14:8-9; Revelation 7:17, 21:1-7

From Deserts to Oceans

Palm Springs was within a couple of hours drive from our home in southern California. Visiting the area for a day trip, we experienced all four seasons in the one day. The township lies in the Mojave Desert where the dry heat can reach 40 degrees Centigrade. In the morning, in our shorts and t-shirts, we marvelled at the drought-resistant cacti and succulents. By the time we arrived at the scenic, forested Lake Arrowhead mountain resort for lunch, we needed long trousers and jumpers. Later we took the aerial tramway up to Mt. San Jacinto, not forgetting to take with us our parkas and gloves. As the cable car made its almost 2000-metre ascent, we admired the sheer cliffs and wooded, snow-covered slopes along the way. At the top we built a mini snowman and enjoyed a snowball fight.

The Earth is a planet of dramatic contrasts. Its surface has dry, hot and barren deserts; temperate fertile valleys with meandering rivers; towering mountains with permanent snow-caps; snow and ice-covered regions with freezing temperatures; humid tropical areas with lush jungles and rain forests; as well as vast oceans lined by sandy beaches and sprinkled with islands and coral reefs. Much of this variation is due to varying amounts and different states of water. Arid areas have minimal rain, while lush rain forests have an abundance. In cold areas, water is semi-permanently frozen.

Water as Type of the Holy Spirit

Water quenches thirst, awakens dormant seeds, sustains life, and cleanses. It cools, comforts and revives a weary person on a scorching day. The Bible uses water as a symbol for the Holy Spirit – the spirit of life, power, love, self-discipline and enlightenment. The Spirit is compared to rain, water springs, and streams of living water. Symbolically, the Spirit can even be "poured out". Like "spiritual water", the Holy Spirit cleanses from sin, imparts eternal life, as well as refreshes, comforts and empowers. Through the power of the Spirit, the dead will be brought back to life. The resurrection is compared to breaking the hard shell of a grain, enabling new life to spring forth.[111]

Water exists in three states – liquid, solid and gas. In a similar way to light, water behaves like both waves and particles. In a rain shower, hailstorm or snowfall, individual "water packages" fall to the earth. On the other hand, a river, lake or ocean consists of an endless series of waves hitting the shore. Like light, water defies some of the established laws of physics and chemistry. Its properties can give a small glimpse into the incomprehensible nature of the Godhead – one God in three simultaneously existing entities, all working in perfect harmony, each with a specific function. The Holy Spirit sometimes acts as a "person" and at other times as a "power" – however, ultimately the Spirit's nature and working are humanly unsearchable.[112]

Throughout the earth's atmosphere, as well as in every living cell, there is a large percentage of water. Moreover, the oceans and other water bodies cover about seventy percent of the earth's surface. Even though only three percent of this is fresh water, ocean water continually evaporates and is moved by air currents over land where it dissipates as fresh water

---

[111] John 4:10-14; 7:37-39; 14:26, 15:26; Acts 10:45; Romans 8:6-11; 1 Corinthians 15:35-38; 42-45; 2 Timothy 1:7
[112] John 3:8; Acts 2:1-4, 16-18; Romans 8:15-16, 26-27; 1 Thessalonians 4:1-8

in the form of rain. Without water, life could not last long.

Similar to water, the Holy Spirit is omnipresent. Having been actively involved in creation, the Spirit is continuously engaged in the sustenance of life. Every living and non-living thing is pervaded by what scientists have recognized as a form of universal energy – even undetectable so-called "dark energy". Without it, life would cease to exist and the physical world would collapse or disappear into nothingness.[113]

The Spirit – Past to Future

In history, the personal involvement of the Holy Spirit in human lives can be seen as mirroring the earth's surface and its amount of water. While the Spirit pervades and sustains all things, as far as directly working with individuals and imparting spiritual understanding and eternal life, it has been just in gentle showers or a few drops – compared to the earth's desert regions. In ancient Israel, very few had the Holy Spirit as an active part of their lives, and in some cases, it was only temporary – for the duration of a certain assigned task. For example, the Spirit imparted special skills to those who worked on the tabernacle or the temple. The Spirit also worked with

---

[113] Genesis 1:1-2; Psalm 104:5-30; 139:7-13

the prophets, as well as some of the kings and leaders. But beyond that, there is little mention of it. Before Jesus' incarnation and death, the Holy Spirit was not generally available. Yet, it was prophesied to be poured out in the "last days", which started with Jesus Christ's first coming to the earth.[114]

The first "Spirit downpour" or "wave" came on the day of Pentecost, fifty days after Jesus' resurrection, when many Jews and proselytes from all parts of the Roman Empire assembled in Jerusalem for the holy day. The Spirit descended with dramatic signs, including mighty wind, tongues of fire, and supernatural understanding of languages, to signify the start of a new era with the new covenant sealed in Christ's blood on the cross. The promised Comforter and Counsellor would now become available to impart eternal life, light and power to those who responded to God's call to come out of the barren desert of the world. The Spirit would empower Christ's disciples to live virtuous lives and fulfil their commission to proclaim his name to the furthermost ends of the earth.[115]

During the church age, there have been other periodic downpours or waves of the Spirit in various

---

[114] Exodus 31:3; Numbers 11:17; Deuteronomy 34:9; Judges 6:34; 11:29; 1 Samuel 10:9-10; 16:13; Joel 2:28-29; Hebrews 1:1; 9:26; 1 Peter 1:20
[115] Acts 1:8; 2:1-21, 38-39; Joel 2:28-32; John 14:16, 26; 15:26; Isaiah 11:1-2

parts of the world, especially when the time was fulfilled for a special event to happen. One such time was when the gospel of the kingdom reached the first Gentile converts.[116] Later, outpourings of the Spirit may have initiated needed reforms or renewal. Typically during these waves, the Holy Spirit moved people to turn or return to the Word of God, and gave new or restored understanding of aspects of the truth. One example was the Protestant Reformation after a period of corruption in the church. Another one was when the Catholic Church made major changes at the Second Vatican Council in the 1960s. These days, the Spirit is moving powerfully in Africa and Asia where many are turning to Christ. Figuratively, during these times of spiritual awakening or rejuvenation, oases in the spiritual desert have sprung up, blossomed, and brought forth fruit as the Spirit enlivened and transformed various communities.

The first Pentecost after Christ's death and resurrection as well as the numerous subsequent revivals were only partial fulfilments of Joel's prophecy about the outpouring of the Holy Spirit. Through them, however, springs and streams of living water have sprung up all over the earth as millions have become born-again children of God and citizens of the heavenly kingdom. Prior to the second coming of Jesus

---

[116] Acts 10:42-48; 11:4-18

Christ, as the good news of salvation is available in all nations, another outpouring of the Spirit is prophesied to occur – and many more will turn to their Creator for deliverance in a time of unprecedented trouble on earth.[117]

The Scriptures speak of a time when the knowledge of God will cover the earth as the waters cover the sea. Spiritual and physical deserts will be transformed into gardens and forests. All will know God who will live among the people. In rich symbolic language, this time is majestically described in the last book of the Bible, the book of Revelation. Satan, the arch-deceiver, will have been removed and forever banished – as will have hate, fighting and wars. The redeemed are pictured in an eternity of glory – a magnificent garden city exists with the tree of life freely available to everyone. And not just one tree of life will be there, but countless ones, full of delicious fruit and healing properties, along the banks of the river of the water of life. At the beginning, humans were banished from the tree of life because of disobedience. At the end, all that was lost as a result of sin will be restored manifold.[118]

---

[117] Romans 8:15-17; Philippians 3:20-21; Matthew 24:21-22; Revelation 7:9-17
[118] Genesis 2:8-9; 3:22-24; Isaiah 11:9; 32:14-18; 35:1-2; 41:18-20; Acts 3:21; Revelation 21:1-6; 22:1-5

Returning to our analogy, we can imagine the Spirit's future action not as a rain shower or even a tropical downpour, but more like a tidal wave or tsunami. It will sweep away the ungodly works of both Satan and humans, and blanket the earth. Instead of deception – compared to salty, undrinkable water of today's oceans – true knowledge and worship of God will pervade the new heavens and earth. Suffering, sickness and death will be history, and the sparkling waters of life will freely flow for everyone to drink. When that happens, Christ's promise of abundant, eternal life will be fulfilled to its ultimate.[119]

---

[119] John 10:10

About the Author

Eva Peck has a Christian and international background. Through Christian work as well as teaching English as a second language in several countries, she has experienced a range of cultures, customs and environments. Having lived and worked in Australia, the United States, Europe, Asia and the Middle East, she now draws on those experiences in her writing.

Eva refers to biblical passages in this book the way she has come to understand them. Having had the opportunity to fellowship with Christians from a variety of faith traditions, she also recognizes that many faith-related issues can be understood in more than one way.

Eva studied both science and theology at the tertiary level and has a Masters degree in Theology. She lives in Brisbane, Australia, with her husband, Alex. The Pecks' other books of spiritual nature include *Pathway to Life – through the Holy Scriptures* and

Journey to the Divine Within – through Silence, Stillness and Simplicity. Both publications, as well as their other books can be ordered online through www.pathway-publishing.org.

More About the Author's Other Books

Divine Reflections in Times and Seasons

This book looks at times and seasons and explores how everyday phenomena mirror spiritual realities. Readers are encouraged to take a fresh look at a sunrise, the sunlight on trees and flowers, the creatures that cross their path, and the starry heavens, among other things, and contemplate the meaning of it all.

Divine Reflections in Living Things

This volume looks at living organisms among both plants and animals and reflects on the glimpses of the divine in these realms.

Divine Insights from Human Experience

This is a collection of writings drawn from the author's experience. Each piece begins with a story and is followed by reflections on the wisdom and/or spiritual insights gleaned from the various incidents. The book consists of two parts – *Wisdom from Life* and *Spiritual Analogies from Life*.

Pathway to Life – Through the Holy Scriptures

Pathway to Life presents in a concise and systematic way the basic teachings of the Bible. It strives to offer a balanced, non-denominational understanding of the Scriptures. Conclusions are supported by scripture references.

Journey to the Divine Within – Through Silence, Stillness and Simplicity

Journey to the Divine Within shares, through the reflections of a variety of spiritual writers, how to enter the realm of one's heart. One way that this occurs is through silence, stillness and simplicity. When pondered, the reflections will lead readers to the silence and stillness of their own hearts on the path to encountering the Life, Light and Love within.

Other Resources

Eva Peck has created several websites with spiritual content. Feel free to browse and explore.

Truth & Beauty
(www.truth-and-beauty.org)

This site seeks to capture what is true and lovely. With the aim of helping readers appreciate the nature of reality, it deals with practical and spiritual aspects of life. To uplift and edify, it provides galleries with beautiful nature images as well as heart-warming stories.

Pathway to Life
(www.pathway-to-life.org)

The site presents the essential Christian message under 36 biblical topics in Q & A style. Where several denominational views exist regarding a subject, these are covered as different interpretations. Supporting scriptures are given throughout. The information is also available in book form.

Heaven's Reflections
(www.heavens-reflections.org)

The site features the theme of seeing the extraordinary in the ordinary, the sacred in the daily, and the special in the routine. It focuses on how the world around us, upon deeper looking, reflects spiritual realities. This book, *Divine Reflections in Natural Phenomena*, is based on the content of the website as are its two companion volumes *Divine Reflections in Times and Seasons* and *Divine Reflections in Living Things*.

You may also enjoy visiting Alexander's websites:

Spirituality for Life
(www.spirituality-for-life.org)

The site shares information with the aim of presenting a practical spirituality to enhance one's life journey and to help fulfil one's divine destiny.

Prayer of the Heart – Journey to the Divine Within
(www.prayer-of-the-heart.org)

This site deals with the prayer of the heart, or meditation, covered from a mainly Christian perspective. It features quotations from a variety of spiritual writers. The content is also available in book form.

See also **www.pathway-publishing.org** for the Pecks' other creations.

Readers' Comments

Thank you kindly for your book series Divine Reflections. I have skimmed through the previews and think that the books are indeed wonderful. I think that your work and words will be an inspiration to the many people that need them in this difficult world in which we are living. You have the experience, knowledge, ability and the spiritual background to reach out to people to give them hope. Well done!
Pauline G., Cairo, Egypt

I have found your book educational, informative and at the same time easy to read. Each time I read one of your books, I am amazed at your knowledge. I have learned many interesting things and have also appreciated the spiritual side of the book. A book like this can be reread over and over.
Liba H., Capalaba, Australia

Your style of writing is very readable and sympathetic, and the way you reflect on the beauties of nature is lovely. Your message and discussion is soft and gentle and makes the reader feel God's love.
Margaret S., Thornlands, Australia

I found your book to be a blend of the cosmic Christ you have discovered in nature and the deep-rooted "word" which is imprinted in your heart.
Sadie M., Thornlands, Australia

The reflections on God's creation were delightful – it is so true, as the Bible tells us in Romans, that we can see the proof of the Creator in His handiwork all around us.
Jan H., Mittagong, Australia

I really liked these reflections and feel like universal truths come through and the words spoken are honest.
Lobat A., Ryiadh, Saudi Arabia

About Pathway Publishing

Pathway Publishing is dedicated to sharing truth and beauty by publishing books that present what is true to life and reality, as well as what is lovely and inspirational. The goal is to not only provide sound information, but also to lift the human spirit.

Pathway Publishing has a vision of helping readers on their path of enlightenment and spiritual transformation. The wisdom and experience of spiritual teachers, thinkers, and visionary writers from various backgrounds and faith traditions are recognized and valued.

Other books produced by Pathway Publishing, beside the *Divine Reflections* trilogy, are:
- *Divine Insights from Human Life,* Eva Peck
- *Pathway to Life - Through the Holy Scriptures,* Eva and Alexander Peck
- *Journey to the Divine Within – Through Silence, Stillness and Simplicity,* Alexander and Eva Peck
- *Artistic Inspirations - Paintings of Jindrich Degen* arranged by Eva and Alexander Peck
- *Floral and Nature Art – Photography of Jindrich Degen* arranged by Eva and Alexander Peck
- *Memories of Times with Dad – Poems and Letters,* Alexander and Eva Peck
- *Volné verše,* Jindrich Degen (in Czech)
- *Verše pro dnešní dobu,* Jindrich Degen (in Czech)

Pathway Publishing
Seeking truth and beauty